GENDÜN CHÖPHEL: PORTRAIT OF A GREAT TIBETAN THINKER

Oral Recollections about Gendün Chöphel

Compiled by
Kirti Rinpoche

Translated by
Yeshi Dhondup

THE LIBRARY OF TIBETAN WORKS & ARCHIVES

Copyright © 2013: Library of Tibetan Works and Archives

ALL RIGHTS RESERVED

No part of this publication may be reproduced, stored in a retrieval system, or transmitted in any form or by any means, electronic, mechanical, photo-copying, recording or otherwise, without the prior permission of the publisher.

ISBN: 978-93-80359-83-0

Published by the Library of Tibetan Works & Archives, Dharamsala, H.P. and printed at Vee Enn Print-O-Pac, New Delhi-1100020.

Contents

Publisher's Note v
Translator's Note vii

Introduction 1
1. What I remember about Gendün Chöphel 27
   Dzongu Nakdo from Amdo
2. My Brief Meeting with Gendün Chöphel 31
   Kazi Lhundup Dorji
3. A Short Narration about Gendün Chöphel 33
   Bhikshu Rigzin Wangpo
4. Gendün Chöphel in My Memory 41
   Rakra Tethong Rinpoche
5. Why was Gendün Chöphel Imprisoned 67
   Kungo Tashi Pelrab
6. Recollections of Gendün Chöphel 89
   Nangra Gedun Zöpa
7. Some Memories of Gendün Chöphel 113
   Narkyi Ngawang Dhondup
8. A Reminiscence of Gendün Chöphel 125
   Alak Jampel
9. A Short True Life Account of Gendün Chöphel 145
   An article by Thönzur Lobzang Tenzin

Bibliography 149
Reference Materials Relating to Life and Works of Gendün Chöphel 151

Publisher's Note

❖

Gendün Chöphel can be credited without doubt as the first modern Tibetan scholar, who pioneered modern research method and literary style in the field of Tibetan literature and historiography. He was also skilled monastic debater, poet and artist. He was very patriotic as well. However, his maverick attitude and unorthodox lifestyle, and his direct challenge to Buddhist scriptures and high lamas on doctrines and views made him a controversial figure. As a result, he was even imprisoned on no clear reason. His profound scholarship, eccentric personality and patriotic sense can be judged from his literary works produced through great hardship, his opinions shared with his students and friends. It is unfortunate that he did not live long and his premature death is a great loss to the country.

Nowadays, more and more educated people, especially Western scholars, are taking an interest in Gendün Chöphel's life story and works. Though his biographies written in Tibetan should be the most important sources, it is not possible for all the Western scholars and non-Tibetan readers to delve in them. Keeping this in view, the Library of Tibetan Works and Archives commissioned Yeshi Dhondup, a staff on the Research and Translation Department of this institution, to make English translation of the *dge 'dun chos 'phel gyi rab byed zhabs btags ma* (Oral Accounts of the Life of Gendün Chöphel), an important source of information about Gendün Chöphel, to make it reach a wider audience, especially the English readers. This book is a collection of oral accounts on Gendün Chöphel collected by the present Kirti Rinpoche when he was serving in the Oral History Department of this library. I am glad that this English version is now available and I want to express my appreciation to Yeshi Dhondup for immediately taking up the task and completing it in time.

Geshe Lhakdor
Director

Translator's Note

❖

It is said, "The first man to compare the cheeks of a young woman to a rose was obviously a poet; the first to repeat it was possibly an idiot." I would be making the same mistake if I described Gendün Chöphel as one of the foremost modern Tibetan intellectuals, a skilled dialectician or a talented painter. To repeat these stereotypical eulogistic descriptions of him would only perpetuate a cliché.

Gendün Chöphel was born in the village of Shopang in Rebkong, Amdo. There is a slight variation in the year of his birth from biography to biography. Rakra Tethong's *Biography of Gendün Chöphel* states that he was born in 1904 or 1905. According to Jeffrey Hopkins' *Tibetan Arts of Love*, Dungkar Lobsang Trinley's *Great Dictionary* and Kirti Rinpoche's *dge 'dun chos 'phel gyi rab 'byed zhabs btags ma*, his birth year was 1903. Sherab Gyatso gives his birth date as 1905. Naga Sangye Tandar, in his article "Life date of Gendün Chöphel" in *Tibet Journal*, vol. 36, suggested 1901 as the year of his birth.

Gendün Chöphel spent his early years at Yama Tashikyil (*g.ya ma bkra shis 'khyil*), the monastic seat of Zhabkar Tsogdruk Rangdrol (*zhabs dkar tshogs drug rang grol*, 1781-1851), who was a proponent of the Rime tradition. At the age of nine, Gendün Chöphel was recognized as the incarnation of a former abbot of Dorji Drak, one of the main Nyingma monasteries in Tibet at the time. He was therefore known as Dodrak Trulku in his early life.

At around the age of 13 he was admitted to a local monastery, Dhitsa Monastery. There he received novice ordination from the 4th

Zhamar Gendün Tenzin Gyatso (1852-1912) and received the name Gendün Chöphel. Two years later, he joined Labrang Tashikyil Monastery, a major monastic centre of Geluk School in Amdo. At Tashikyil, he earned a reputation as an expert in the art of dialectics as well as for his extensive scriptural knowledge. At the same time, he earned a negative reputation for his criticism of the texts used in the monastery's curriculum and for his unorthodox attitude, as well as his friendship with an American missionary, the Reverend Marion Griebenow, who was not popular with the monastic community. From Marion Griebenow he learned some basics of English and techniques of making mechanical toys. He once made a toy boat and sent it across the Sangchu River, amazing all other monks.

Soon he had to face criticism from other monks, especially senior monks and authorities of the monastery. Finally, he left the monastery for Lhasa in 1926 and joined Drepung Monastery. There he became a disciple of Geshe Sherab Gyatso (1884-1968), a renowned monk scholar of the time, but their teacher-disciple relationship soon became strained, as Gendün Chöphel often used to find fault with the Buddhist doctrines and even challenged his teacher on religious topics. Irritated by his student's behaviour, Sherab Gyatso refused to address him by his name, instead calling him "mad man," which inspired the title of Donald S. Lopez's biography of Gendün Chöphel *The Madman's Middle Way: Reflections on Reality of the Tibetan Monk Gendün Chöphel.*

In 1934, Gendün Chöphel met the Indian scholar Rahul Sankrityayan (1893-1963), who had come to Tibet for the second time disguised as a Buddhist monk, with the aim of collecting ancient Sanskrit manuscripts that had been brought from India. They became friends and went together to search for Indian manuscripts in various monasteries and temples in Tibet. When Rahul returned to India, he seized the opportunity to fulfill his longtime wish to visit India, and he went with him. He was 32 years old then. His visit to India stimulated his inquisitive mind and expanded his scholarship. He spent about twelve years in India, touring across the country, visiting cities, sacred places, archaeological sites and even brothels.

He met the Russian scholar George Roerich and helped him translate Gö Lotsawa Zhonu Pel's *deb ther sngon po* (*Blue Annals*) but sadly, no credit was given to Gendün Chöphel in the acknowledgements. He also helped Jacques Bacot (1877-1965) in studying the Old Tibetan Dunhuang manuscripts, and Bacot published the results in 1940 but did not acknowledge Gendün Chöphel's help. In India, he was prolific writer; he composed many works and translated many Indian Buddhist or non-Buddhist texts into Tibetan. The most remarkable among them was *rgyal khams rig pas bskor ba'i gtam rgyud gser gyi thang ma* (Accounts of Pilgrimage to Various Sacred Places in Tibet and India), which is his masterpiece and most important and lasting contribution to the Tibetan literature.

He joined the Maha Bodhi Society, an international Buddhist missionary organization, which funded his trip to Sri Lanka where he learned Pali. He visited different Buddhist sacred places in the country and composed the *Guide to Sacred Places in Sri Lanka* and *History of Sri Lanka*. The latter one was so beautifully written that it is suitable to readers of any level, and it gives very picturesque descriptions of the country and its people and culture.

The 13th Dalai Lama wrote to a Bhutanese official Draksho Dorji requesting him to translate one of Tsongkhapa's writing into English and he in turn sought Gendün Chöphel's help. They jointly finished the work in two months period. With the help of Raja Dorji, he took a tour to Bhutan and wrote a Bhutan travelogue with illustrations, including maps. The Bhutanese government sent a complaint to the Tibetan government against his activities.

In Kalimpong, he met Rabga Pandatsang, a Tibetan political fugitive, who had founded a political party so-called "Nub Bö Lekcho Tsokpa" (*nub bod legs bcos tshogs pa*), whose official English title was the "Tibet Improvement Party." The members included Changlochen Gung, Bapa Phuntsok Wangyal and Khunphel-la. Whether he was a member of the Party is still the subject of controversy. The logo of the organization, which looked similar to a Russian logo, was devised by him. He received monthly payment from Rabga. He made a map of Bhutan for the Party. He also studied socialism with a relative of George

Roerich. These clues would make a casual enquiry or precipitous judgment to suggest he belonged to the Party. However, given his strong nationalistic feeling and indifference towards wealth, it is very difficult to believe it.

After twelve years in India, he returned to Tibet in 1946, with loads of notes and manuscripts, a mass of experience and a broader mental horizon. He began composing a Tibetan history, the *White Annals*, based on the Dunhuang documents and Chinese annals, as well on notes made during his visits to various monuments and archeological sites in India and Tibet. However, he could not complete it as he imprisoned by the government. He also composed a very controversial but a masterpiece work entitled *Ornament to Nagarjuna's Intent*, in which he has criticized Nagarjuna's doctrine of the Middle Way. This work depicts his high standard scholarship and profound knowledge of both sutra and tantra, and his precise understanding of the teachings of the Buddha and intents of Nargarjuna. The members of the Geluk School strongly criticized the work, but their criticisms were more or less a personal attack on him rather than arguments against his views expressed in the book. Some Geluk members who were his friends or sympathizers, on the other hand, did not want the text to be attributed to him, and blamed his student Dawa Zangpo for the text, although they knew that such a highly scholastic work could be composed only by Gendün Chöphel, not by his student Dawa Zangpo.

In 1947, Gendün Chöphel was arrested and imprisoned by the Tibetan government on the false charge of counterfeiting Tibetan 100-rupee notes and circulating them in Lhasa, and all his manuscripts and other research materials were seized, never to be returned. He was released in 1950 along with all the other prisoners during the amnesty to celebrate the 14th Dalai Lama's assumption of full political and spiritual responsibility for Tibet. Gendün Chöphel blamed Richardson, the British Political Representative in Lhasa, but the latter denied having a hand in the former's imprisonment. The British government of India most likely sent a report to the Tibetan government about the doubtful activities of Gendün Chöphel and his friendship with Pomda Rabga and Changlochen Gung who were out of favour with the Tibetan government at that time. The Tibetan authorities hazily acted and showed off their power on an innocent man, who was dedicated towards his country and compatriots. Blinded by ignorance they failed to understand his profound scholarship and nationalistic sense.

This tragic event destroyed both Gendün Chöphel's spirit and scholastic career. After his release from prison, finding all his notes and manuscripts missing from his house, he fell into deep depression and became mentally unstable. He started drinking and smoking excessively and behaving abnormally. He stopped studying and writing. Had the government returned his notes and manuscripts and rehabilitated him, he would have continued with his work and we would have been lucky enough to see the *White Annals* in it complete form as the first comprehensive Tibetan history book. He would have left for us a legacy of many more highly refined works. Unfortunately, this did not happen. Gendün Chöphel succumbed to his illness in 1951, one year after his release from prison.

He lived a life of an impoverished man. He called himself "learned pauper." Considering his extensive knowledge, exceptional ability in dialectics and talent for both traditional *thangka* painting and modern arts, Gendün Chöphel could have lived a luxurious life, but he spent his whole life in the quest of knowledge and doing academic works, surviving on the small amount of money he received as offerings or gifts from his patrons, students and friends. When he arrived back in Tibet, the only belongings he brought with him were boxes of manuscripts, texts and notes written on scraps of papers, cigarette wrappers, etc. He was a scholar in the true sense of the word. He was a real Mahayana practitioner. The gist of his life can be understood from this poem, which he wrote just before his death:

> I did not marry and keep a wife in my youth,
> Nor did I amass wealth that I need in old age;
> I, an impoverished man, am going to die sorrowfully
> Holding a fountain pen in my hand!

Nowadays, he is remembered with great remorse by many Tibetans. In Tibet, an art gallery called Gendün Chöphel Artists' Guild has been opened in his name. The Amnye Machen Institute, Dharamsala, has instituted an award called Gendün Chöphel Award to be presented every three years to an outstanding Tibetan writer who has maintained dedication and courage in the face of persecution and hardship. The Award carries a cash prize and framed citation. His works are compiled and published. Books are written and films are made on his life. Many Western scholars are taking an interest in his life accounts. This volume contains recollections about Gendün Chöphel narrated by people who had known Gendün Chöphel closely or less intimately at various times during his life or had first-hand information about him. Compiled by the 11th Kirti Rinpoche, it was published in 1983 by the Library of Tibetan Works and Archives. Kirti Rinpoche later revised the book by adding quotes from different Tibetan sources on Gendün Chöphel and including his photos, portraits, handwriting samples, and articles and paintings done by him. The revised Tibetan version was published by the Kirti Monastery in 2003. This English translation is based on the original version published by the Library in 1983.

In conclusion, I want to dedicate this work to all those intellectuals in the world who suffered the same fate suffered by Gendün Chöphel. Finally, I would like to express my sincere thanks to Ms. Kerry Wright (Australia) and Ms. Gill Winter (New Zealand) for checking the English and making the necessary corrections. I also want to thank Geshe Lhakdor-la, Director of the Library of Tibetan Works and Archives, for the publication of this book.

Yeshi Dhondup

Bibliography

Childs, Geoff. "Perceptions of Relative Wealth in a Tibetan Community: A Note on Research Methodology." *Tibet Journal,* vol. ii, Dharamasala, LTWA.

--------. Names and Nicknames in Skyi grong". *Tibet Journal,* vol. 28.3, Dharamsala LTWA.

Duncan, Marion H. *Customs and Superstitions of Tibetans.* Kathmandu: Pilgrims Publications.

Pemba, Lhamo. Tibetan Proverbs. Dharamsala: LTWA

Stein, R. A. *Tibetan Civilization.* California: Stanford University Press, 1972.

Chophel, Norbu. *Folk Tales of Tibet.* Dharamsala: Library of Tibetan Works & Archives, 1984.

Harrer, Heinrich. *Seven Years in Tibet. Translated from the German by Richard Graves. With an introduction by Peter Fleming,* First Tarcher/Putnam Hardcover Edition, 1997.

Gyamtso, Palden Tsering. *The History, Religion, Culture and Traditions of Bhutia Communities,* Sikkim: Shomoon House, 2010.

Chöphel, Gendün. *Tibetan Arts of Love.* English translation by Jeffrey Hopkins. New York: Snow Lion Publications

Introduction

❖

The 20th century witnessed the emergence of the great Tibetan scholar, Gendün Chöphel, whose absence now is felt with a great sense of remorse not only by scholars, but also by ignorant people who believe in popular rumours. However, when this great scholar was alive, he was made a victim of false accusations and subjected to extreme torture, and he finally died, stricken with grief. Although his misfortune certainly resulted from causal karmic factors, there were also immediate factors that played a role. Because he expressed his views on Buddhist or non-Buddhist topics openly without restrain by reasoning instead of accepting others' views, and his unexcelled skill in the field of exposition, debate and composition, some self-proclaimed scholars spread negative rumours about him, out of jealousy. Besides, because of his heterodox attitudes, some orthodox minded people taunted him a lot, either calling him "non-Buddhist" or criticizing him for not treating the teachings of the Buddha and past Buddhist masters as true and standard, or adulterating the sublime Dharma and contravening its precepts and commitments. For example, it was said, "As everyone in Tibet has heard, when Gendün Chöphel was in Tibet, he criticized Je Tsongkhapa's middle-way philosophy as flawed, all the works of the early translators as inaccurate, Nagarjuna's views as invalid and so on. The central government [of Tibet] must arrest this enemy of Buddhadharma.(i)."

When Gendün Chöphel was imprisoned, others took advantage of the situation and tried hard to tarnish his image. Even his writings were subjected to derision out of jealousy, as is clear from this verse written by him:

> In a forest filled with the thundering roars
> Of furious tigers craving for blood,
> A child of truth, who is left alone,
> Is an object of compassion to learned people.(ii)

Gendün Chöphel sensed the drastic consequences Tibet would face if it did not take steps in pace with the developments that were taking place all over the world. He therefore often talked about the need for change and progress in Tibet. At that time, since he was associated with Pomda Rabga[1], Chensel Kunphel[2] and Changlochen Gung[3], who were out of favour with some high Tibetan government officials, he was suspected of planning to introduce communism in Tibet. The Tibetan public easily believed the rumour. Some foreigners meddled in the affair against him. The Tibetan government announced his arrest, accusing him of committing the serious crime of counterfeiting Tibetan 100-rupee notes. As a result, he went through years of torment. However, since the truth by its very nature always prevails, his fame grows like the waxing of the moon, as the way of thinking of Tibetan people progresses.

His rise to fame

Gendün Chöphel was already popular in his youth. He was innately intelligent and diligent, and had an exceptional talent for debate and dialectics. He was also skilled in drawing and had a great memory. By virtue of these qualities, in Domé everybody called him "Dhitsa Alak"(iii), "Dhitsa Kampo," "Dodrak Tülku"(iv) or "Dodrak Gendün Chöphel". Later, when he joined Gomang College at Drepung Monastery, his skills in logic and dialectics greatly impressed the learned monks, and he was regarded as the epitome of brilliance.

Later on he travelled to India and Sri Lanka, and translated some important treatises which had not been translated into Tibetan before. He composed many works such as *Guide to the Sacred Places in India*.

His work called *White Annals* in particular ushered in the beginning of a new form of Tibetan historiography. In the homage verses of his *White Annals*, he wrote:

> Having compiled the accurate statements and clear chronologies
> Recorded in the available old documents,
> I have gained the confidence to make a small appraisal
> Of the political status and powers of the early Tibetan empire.(v)

He gave a lucid account of the Tibetan imperial period more than a thousand years ago, that was not found in the works of earlier Tibetan writers. He confirmed the dates of King Songtsen Gampo's birth and death, and he became popular in western academic circles. Commenting on his style of writing, he once wrote:

> I am not a meek fool who believes in whatever is heard. I am a wise pauper, endowed with innate intelligence, who has spent all his life in accumulating knowledge. Therefore, one should not think whatever I say is untrue, baseless and deceptive. For most people, if a person explains a complex idea in a simplified manner, he is not taken seriously or is scorned. On the other hand, if a simple thing is presented in a complicated manner, he is considered learned. I am helpless now.(vi)

Gendün Chöphel based his research on facts, using logic and modern research methods, and confirmed the findings. In this way, he became famous.

Gendün Chöphel's heterodoxy versus Tibetan society at the time

Gendün Chöphel's views had no place in orthodox Tibetan society. It was therefore natural that he faced many problems wherever he went in Tibet. For instance, when he was at Tashikhyil Monastery (Amdo), there were many brilliant students in his class, including his friend Yiga Jamyang. Once when the two were discussing the credibility of the monastery's curricular texts, some elder monks of the monastery overheard them. The monks became angry and started annoying the two, ultimately forcing Gendün Chöphel to flee to Ü-Tsang and Yiga Jamyang to Taktsang Lhamo. A rumour circulated that the two had to leave the monastery because they were unable to withstand the wrath of the Dharma protectors, but I do not know whether it was true or not. The following is an alphabetic poem *(ka bshad)* in the Amdo dialect composed by Gendün Chöphel, probably after leaving Tashikhyil Monastery, intended to clarify the negative rumours about him that spread after he had left the monastery.

> Hey! After I have left
> Some elderly monks who had no control over their mouths
> Said that Nechung, the King of Excellent Activities,
> Forced me to leave because I was arrogant.
>
> If the Dharma Protector really exists,
> Would it let worthless people
> Who travel to known and unknown lands
> To do trade in tea, alcohol, food and animals to remain there?
>
> Those who wear robes by folding (them) up from below like the leaves of the plantain
> (And) carry inferior instruments such as clubs and knives
> Should be expelled to other places;
> But their number increases year by year.
>
> Some say that I was expelled
> Because I lack faith like the planet Venus.
> If so, why then are the lower beings
> Such as cows, oxen, *zomos*[4], birds, insects not evicted?
>
> The four-fanged King Nechung has no reasons
> To expel in an improper manner
> Those who study the texts of the Dza-ya (the Victorious One),
> Bearing all difficulties—heat and cold, trials and hardship.
>
> Mischievous [people] who wear expensive robes, hats and shoes, and
> Mischievous [people] who live on poor and paltry food
> May look very different to our eyes,
> But they appear no different to the Victor above.

Rather than banishing those who are proud of knowing
The texts of Ra *(ra bsdus)* and the Se texts *(bse bsdus)*,
Wouldn't it be better to banish those arrogant people
Who trade in meat, alcohol and animals to other lands.

Ha, Ha! Think for yourself if this is true.
Ask the elderly geshes properly.
I, Sangha Dharma, the King of Reasoning, say so.(vii)

(It is said that this poem was sent to Labrang when he was on his way to Lhasa.)

While at the monastery, he and his classmates coined many new terms, and also devised a code language by reversing sentences, to the confusion of others. For example, the sentence "khyed rang gang du pheb kyi yod dam/" (Where are you going?) was changed to "dam yod kyi pheb du gang rang khyed/"(viii)

Those who did not like the use of such a language derided and nicknamed the class "Terminology Class" or "those who speak in a devil's language". When in Ü-Tsang, Gendün Chöphel was labeled "heretic," "communist," "criminal," and so forth. It is clear that all these labels and the public's bad opinion of Gendün Chöphel can be attributed mainly to his heterodoxy.

HIS ACTIVITIES IN INDIA

Gendün Chöphel's friendship with Rahul [Sankrityayan], a great Indian scholar, and his interest in learning Sanskrit and English took him to India. He once wrote, "Until I have learned a little Sanskrit and the foreign language (English), I will not leave India."(ix)

He first went to Chakong in Sikkim and learnt English from a monk named Jonoras. Later he taught Tibetan at the Y.M.B.A School (Young Men's Buddhist Association) founded by Jonoras in a Tibetan village in Darjeeling.(x) Having arrived in India in 1934 or 1935, within a short time he gained proficiency in the Sanskrit and English languages up to a level at which he could translate from and into these languages. (xi) This is evident from his English translation of the Buddhist text *Engaging in the Bodhisattva's Way of Life* and his Tibetan translations of the *Ramayana* and *Shakuntala* made around 1936. His other literary works undertaken during his stay in India are as follows:

1. In 1937, he composed *Guide to the Sacred Places in India* in Varanasi.
2. In 1938, he composed *Arts of Lovemaking* in Mathura *(bcom rlag)*.
3. In 1941, he translated the *Bhagavad Gita* in Tibetan.
4. In 1944, while in Sri Lanka, he translated *Dhammapada*.
5. In the winter of 1944, in Kullu he composed an article called "About the Tibetan Letters *ca* and *cha*".
6. In 1945, he revised and expanded the *Guide to the Sacred Places in India*.
7. In 1946, he started composing the *White Annals*.
8. At Kullu, he translated the *Blue Annals* in collaboration with George Roerich

Although it is certain that he composed or translated many works in India during his more than 12 years' stay there, the above mentioned are the only works that I have come to know about.

Gendün Chöphel once wrote,

> Through the rays of pure love for my people
> That glow spontaneously from the core of my heart,
> I have done a little service out of my great efforts
> To the kings and people of my land of snow.(xii)

Gendün Chöphel faced great financial problems, making his life more difficult. In one of his letters, he wrote, "Though I have a strong desire to return home, it is difficult for me since I have no money now. It really makes me sad. I feel money is the only God (ori.) of this world."(xiii) In another letter, he said, "I want to go to Darjeeling, but I have no money. What is the best thing to do? Can I get some money from my paintings?"(xiv) He further wrote, "If I get a job in a school in Patna, it would help me. I am penniless and I find it extremely difficult."(xv)

Reading between the lines, Gendün Chöphel was right in calling himself "a learned pauper."

GENDÜN CHÖPHEL RETURNS TO TIBET

It appears that Gendün Chöphel's close connection with Pomda Rabga and his associates, who were in those days rumoured to be starting revolutionary movements (in Tibet), and others who were staunch supporters of communism displeased the British government of India. The mistrust between him and the British government (xvi) was very apparent, as he once wrote, "Be cautious with the blonde monkeys!"(xvii) The misunderstanding between the two deepened further when the British government seized a map from him which he had prepared on his way back to Tibet via Bhutan.(xviii) As soon as he arrived in Lhasa by way of Lhoka, many educated and uneducated people, who were infatuated with him, competed to have the honour of being his host.

Later some foreigners intentionally spread a bad rumour against him. Some high Tibetan government officials and educated people who were jealous of him and ordinary ignorant people accepted the rumour as truth. They called him "communist" and "blasphemous." In 1947, the government arrested him on a false charge of counterfeiting 100-rupee currency notes. Gendün Chöphel exclaimed with shock, "Don't put the blame on me for the crimes you have committed!"(xix)

Gendün Chöphel was subjected to harsh or mild interrogation lasting for many hours several times. He was kept in Zhöl prison for a long time without being convicted. Cabinet minister Kashöpa, who arrested Gendün Chöphel, later advised Lubum Section of Drepung Monastery about how to secure his release. Therefore, the following street song became popular in Lhasa at that time:

> Kashö, who is a damaru (drum)[5],
> Swindled the case like a pot of *thugpa* (noodles in soup).[6]

This shows that Kashöpa had double faces(metaphor). Gendün Chöphel suffered much in prison and was released either at the end of 1948 or the beginning of 1949 on bail signed by Lubum Section of Drepung Monastery, on the condition that he was to be handed back to the government whenever ordered. His case was not closed.(xx)

A few months later, the government requested him to write a book on Tibetan history, with a promise to give him a salary in the form of cash or ration, plus accommodation. However, greatly disheartened by the severe accusations made against him, he took to excessive drinking and (xxi) started behaving strangely. He could not complete his Tibetan history. He soon became ill and succumbed to his illness in 1951.(xxii)

His religious beliefs

It appears that although Gendün Chöphel pursued most of his formal religious studies in Gelukpa monasteries, he had a natural affinity towards the Nyingmapa tradition. It was said that his father was a Nyingma tantric practitioner, and he himself was recognised as the reincarnation of a Nyingmapa master. Both Jigmé Samten Rinpoche and his spiritual son used to refer to him as "Dodrak Tülku" or "Dodrak Gendün Chöphel." As a genuine learned man, he perceived all the different Buddhist schools as the same and did not attach himself to any one philosophical view or standpoint and criticize others.(xxiii)

It was customary for all traditional scholars to propound a theory by means of the three-fold step—refutation [of others' views], establishment [of one's own theory] and response [to others' criticisms]. This is found everywhere in the approach maintained by the followers of the four major Buddhist schools of thought in India and the four Tibetan Buddhist traditions—Nyingma, Sakya, Kagyü and Geluk. Every individual monastery follows its own set of treatises by refuting the false views of others, establishing correct views of oneself and avoiding invalid responses. Therefore, Gendün Chöphel may have practised the same method occasionally.

Gendün Chöphel's life coincided with the period when people misused religion as an instrument to attack others. He was rumoured to be a heretic and against the Gelukpa tradition, throwing the general public into total confusion.(xxiv) However, he strictly professed all the Buddhist traditions without discrimination, and he was a saint who practised the pure Dharma, as we know from his writings and biographies.

WAS GENDÜN CHÖPHEL A COMMUNIST? AN ATHEIST?

While in Darjeeling, Gendün Chöphel became good friends with the family of Draya Dolma Yangzom and her two husbands—a Tibetan husband from Amdo and a communist western husband.(xxv) He stayed in their house as a guest for a long time. He developed a very warm friendship with the Indian scholar Rahul [Sankriyayana], who also supported communist thoughts. Furthermore, he not only became close to Russian scholar George Roerich (1902-1961), but also studied Marxism with one of Roerich's female acquaintances. From these we can surmise that he was greatly interested in the ideals of Marxism.

At one time, his behaviour displeased Babu Tharchin, who had a close connection with an intelligence agent of the British government of India. This and many of the factors mentioned above made the British government of India suspect that he was a Russian spy.(xxvi)

Gendün Chöphel felt that unless Tibet welcomed change and reforms, the country would not be able to maintain its nationhood. Driven by his great love for his country and people, he intrepidly and fearlessly expressed his views and suggestions on the Tibetan governmental system. (xxvii)

With the spread of communism in the world, Tibet witnessed its neighbouring countries suffering persecution of their religion and culture under the fast growing communist movements. Furthermore, in his last testament, the Thirteenth Dalai Lama had predicted that communism would spread in Tibet. For these reasons, the general populace of Tibet viewed communists as the enemy of the Dharma.

The Tibetan people regarded 'communist,' 'communism' and 'reform movement' as the same and there were hardly anyone who knew the differences between them. Therefore, people with vested interests purposely spread negative rumours of Gendün Chöphel being a 'communist' and 'heretic' to confuse the public. On the contrary,

Gendün Chöphel was a staunch admirer of progress and reforms, but not a communist. He was not involved in political activities.

How I collected information about Gendün Chöphel

When I was in my native region in Tibet, I heard of "Dhitsa Kampo", meaning "a thin monk from Dhitsa", and had a slight interest in him. Later when I joined the Library of Tibetan Works & Archives in Dharamsala, I was entrusted with the task of collecting Gendün Chöphel's works and accounts of his life. Having located all the places that he had visited or stayed, I traveled to all of them and conducted field research. I met with the people whom Gendün Chöphel had known and befriended and interviewed them about his life. The following is a brief report on my research.

1. During his stay at Chakong in Sikkim, Gendün Chöphel learned English from a monk named Jonoras, who also provided him with accommodation and food. I went to Jonara's house where I met his brother Kazi Lhundup Dorji, who told me that Jonoras and Gendün Chöphel jointly translated the *Engaging in the Bodhisattva's Way of Life* into English. He further told me that the book was kept in Jonoras' house in a Tibetan village in Darjeeling.
2. At the suggestion of Kachen Lhakdor of Tashi Lhunpo, who shared accommodation with Gendün Chöphel in Sikkim for some time, I visited the Y.M.B.A School in a small Tibetan village in Darjeeling where Jonoras and Gendün Chöphel resided together. I made an inquiry at the school's office about Gendün Chöphel, but the staff did not know anything about him. In one of the office cabinets, I found the original copy of the *Bodhicarya Avatara* translated into English.
3. In Darjeeling, Amdo Gönlung Gyatso guided me to the home of Draya Dolma Yangzom's daughter Lhatso. She remembered Gendün Chöphel giving her mother a collection of poems advice in verses written in Kullu and a scroll-painting of Vaishravana. He had also made paintings on their altar, but the paintings were not in a good state of preservation. She recalled how Gendün Chöphel, whom she used to call "Lubum Lhadri

(Artist from Lubum)," would wrap himself in a blanket while making these paintings.
4. Also in Darjeeling, with the help of Zhimé Chondzé *(gzhis smad chos mdzad)*, I went to the house of Kamala, the last wife of Rahul. When asked about Gendün Chöphel, she gave me some letters written in English, Tibetan and Sanskrit, addressed to Rahul, carrying Gendün Chöphel's signature, and two collections of verses of advice in the Tibetan language. She also had a photo of Gendün Chöphel taken in Sakya with a caption by Rahul. She kindly gave me all these items.
5. I travelled to Chakong in Sikkim where Gendün Chöphel translated the *Ramayana* into Tibetan. There I met Jonoras' younger brother, but he knew nothing about Gendün Chöphel. I did not find anything related to Gendün Chöphel there.
6. With the help of Gelong Rigzin Wangpo and Sonam Tsewang who were Tharchin Babu's relative and secretary respectively, I was able to find several works by Gendün Chöphel, including the original manuscripts of "About Gemstone Keta", "Water and Tree", "Description of Champaka Flower" and "Description of Udumvara Flower" written in his own handwriting. There was also an unpublished original article written in protest against the imprisonment of Gendün Chöphel submitted to the press, and many press clippings containing columns and articles by Gendün Chöphel. I also found a portrait of Rina Athing with Gendün Chöphel's signature on the bottom. (The house in which Gendün Chöphel lived during his stay in Kalimpong lay in ruins at the time.)
7. Gelong Rinzin Wangpo furnished me with handwritten copies of the articles "About the Tibetan Letters Ca and Cha" and "Natural Transfiguration of U-chen to U-mé" as well as a copy of a letter written by Gendün Chöphel to Tharchin Babu, an unfinished copy of *Guide to the Sacred Places in India* and a painting of Buddha Shakyamuni, which bore the signature of Gendün Chöphel.
8. Interviewed Dzongu Nakdo from Amdo, who knew much about Gendün Chöphel's birthplace and life.
9. Interviewed Rakra Rinpoche, who studied under Gendün Chöphel when the latter arrived in Tibet from India.

10. Interviewed Gelong Rinzin Wangpo, a close colleague of Gendün Chöphel before the latter was imprisoned by the Tibetan government.
11. Interviewed Tashi Pelrab, the officer in charge at Nangtseshak Prison, about Gendün Chöphel's life in prison and later.
12. Interviewed Amdo Nangra Gendün Zöpa, who was specially appointed by Lubum Khangtsen of Drepung Monastery to obtain the release of Gendün Chöphel.
13. Interviewed Alak Jampel, who became close to Gendün Chöphel after he was released from prison.
14. Interviewed Narkyi Ngawang Dhondup, one of the few students of Gendün Chöphel in his last years.

CHRONOLOGY OF GENDÜN CHÖPHEL'S LIFE BASED ON VARIOUS SOURCES

1902 (Newfound date)
Samdong Rinpoche Lobzang Tenzin:
   Given that he was 32 years old when he visited India in 1934, the Wood-Dog year of the 16th *Rabjung* Cycle, it is certain that he was born in 1902, the Water-Tiger year of the 15th Rabjung Cycle.

1903
Horkhang Sonam Pelbar:
   He was born the son of a Tantric practitioner named Dorji, who was also known as Alak Gyalpo, and his mother, Pema in the Water-Female Rabbit year.

1905
   Amdo Gendün Chöphel was born in Zhöma village at Shongpang, in the Rebkong region of Amdo.

1911
   When Gendün Chöphel was seven years old, his father died.

1917
Horkhang Sonam Pelbar:
   In the Fire-Snake year, at around 15 years of age, he studied basic logic at

Dhitsa Monastery, the monastery of Zhamar Pandita.

1923

Dorji Gyal:
Towards the end of his 19th year, he joined the great monastery Labrang Tashikhyil.

1927

At the age of 23, Gendün Chöphel sought formal admission to Drepung Gomang Monastery.

1929

Dorji Gyal:
Leaving Labrang Monastery, Gendün Chöphel arrived at his birthplace Showong. On the 26th day of the 8th month, at the age of 25, he composed "Holder of Lotus, the One Who Embodies Compassion" and others.

1934

After spending seven years in the monastery, he left for India with Rahul, by way of Sakya and others.

1934

In the conclusion of the *Guide to the Sacred Places in India* composed in 1945, Gendün Chöphel wrote:
"This is a revised and extended version of the guide, which I wrote 12 years after I arrived in India."

1934

The Golden Chronicle, the Story of a Cosmopolitan's Pilgrimage[7]
"In the Wood-Male-Dog year of the 16th *Rabjung* cycle, when I was 32, I left for India." Also, "Passing through Nyanang, I finally reached Nepal."

1934

In *The Golden Chronicle*, Gendün Chöphel wrote:
"At age of 32, on the 18th day of the last winter month, I drank water from the River Ganga."

Tibet Mirror, 1 December 1951 (5th day of the 10th month of the 925th *Rablo* year)[8], issue no. 9.
"During his 12 stay in India, the land of superior beings...."

1 Jan 1935
Personal correspondence
(A Sanskrit correspondence written in Tibetan script)
Tav tatra (English) stoka samskrita//
Ca pathami anya kopikaryam nastiti//

6 July 1935
Personal correspondence:
> Currently, I am in Darjeeling. I find no new teacher to teach me new Sanskrit lessons, but I am doing the revision of the texts that I had studied before. I am also studying the foreign language (English). I am thinking of going to Nepal to study Sanskrit from Brahmin Prasannajit and work some time.

8 Sept 1935
Personal correspondence:
> I am at Jonoras' house in Darjeeling. Although it is quite difficult, he is providing me with food and other things. In the meantime, I finished studying three or four English textbooks. Unable to find teachers, I have not been able to do further study in Sanskrit. I am planning to stay in India for two or three years and study Sanskrit and English

15 Dec 1935
Personal correspondence:
> I started off to go to the monk's (Jonoras') former residence in Chakong, a village 15 miles from Darjeeling. If I fail to return to Tibet by the summer of next year, I will continue my English courses at Darjeeling. Until I gain an adequate knowledge of English and Sanskrit, I prefer not to leave India.

14 Jan 1936
Personal correspondence:
> "I am currently staying at a small village called Chakong. I am planning to translate the *Shakuntala-natakam*, but I am not able to do this at present. Although I very much desire to return to my native land, I cannot do so for I have no money. I really feel sad. Money is the only God of the universe. With Jonoras' help, I have been able to make notable improvements with my English."

7 Feb 1936
Personal correspondence: (original)

"...I LEARNED SOME ENGLISH SINCE LAST YEAR. NOW I AM ABLE TO WRITE SOME WORDS HARDLY, BUT MY PRONUNCIATION IS STILL WORSE, AS ENGLISH IS THE OPPOSITE TO བོད་སྐད། I HAVE BEEN TRANSLATING THE IMPORTANT TEXT OF RAMAYANA WITH MR. NORGYA WHO KNOWS THREE LANGUAGES WELL. IF IT FINISHES, I THINK IT MUST BE A HELP TO MANY ROOTS OF THE OLD བོད་ཀྱི་བསྟན་བཅོས། CLEARLY. AND STILL I LONG MOST TO TRANSLATE ཤཀུནྟ་ལཱ་ WITH THE HELP OF YOUR HONOUR, AND I CAN PROMISE TO MAKE IT AS BEAUTIFULL LINE AS A GREAT TIBETAN HAS DONE, AND NEVER DEFILE YOUR BRIGHT FAME. PLEASE LET ME KNOW HOW IS YOUR HEALTH NOW. I AM KEEPING QUITE WELL. WITH MY HEALTH. NAMASKAR. I SENT HIM SOME STORY ABOUT ཨེ་ and སྰཾ IN ASHOKA'S LETTER AND HE WAS VERY VERY PLEASED.

12 Feb 1936

If I get a job in Patna University, it will help me greatly. I am facing great financial problems. Nowadays, I am in a small village in Sikkim, and I am planning to go to Darjeeling next month. I am presently working on the *Ramayana*. I very much want to translate the *Shakuntala-natakam*, if you like. If others translate this, I am sure they will find it quite hard to get equivalent terms and expressions.

12 March 1936
Personal correspondence:

I have also sent a letter to the Samlo section's Geshe in Nepal. Kindly enclose the Geshe Sherab's letter for me with your letter.

31 March 1936
Personal correspondence:

I am studying English. Though I can write a little, I still find it hard to speak.

29 May 1936
Personal correspondence

I am staying with the venerable Jonoras in Darjeeling studying as before.

1936
> This second volume of collection of advice in Tibetan verses was done by the great Indian pandit Rahul Sanktriyayan, a master of Buddhist Tripitaka, Domépa Gendün Chöphel and Nono Tseten from Maryul. In the preface, it says, "This text was composed in collaboration with spiritual friend Gendün Chöphel in the 2480th year after *mahaparinirvana* of Lord Buddha, in the city of Patliputra of central India.

1 Nov 1937 "I have now decided to live in Kalimpong. Although I received many letters from the venerable Jonoras calling me to Darjeeling, I must stay here (in Kalimpong) for a few months."

1937
> "This text of a *Guide to Sacred Places in India* was composed by the alms-seeker Gendün Chöphel at Saranath in the Fire-Female year."

1938 Dorji Gyal:
> He [Gendün Chöphel] wrote a letter to his mother and other relatives on the 30th day of the 2nd month of the Earth-Male Tiger year.

1938
In translator's note of the *Arts of Lovemaking:*
> "This was composed by Gendün Chöphel, the one who has cleared all doubts over all that can be seen, heard or experienced about sex, desire and lust, at the residence of my lady friend Ganga in Mathura near the bank of the Yamuna in the late mid-winter of the Tiger year."

1939
> "In the Spring of the Hare year, I wrote wrote the *Shakuntala-natakam* in Tibetan calligraphy during my stay at Patliputra."

1941
> "*Bhagavad Gita's* 12th chapter titled "Bhakti Yoga" (The Path of Devotion) was translated into Tibetan by the alms-seeker Gendün Chöphel with the help of Swami Buddhan, on the 4th day of the 4th month of the Iron-Snake year of the 16th *Rabjung* Cycle."

1942
Dorji Gyal:
> In the Water-Horse year of the 16th *Rabjung* Cycle, he went to Calcutta, the place associated with the deity Mahakala. There he worked at the Mahabodhi Society of India.14

15 July 1944
   This (Tibetan) translation of the Dhammapada text was completed by Gendün Chöphel at Pel Reldri Riwo Gön (Sinhalese temple meaning the 'Temple of Sword Mountain') in Sri Lanka in the Wooden-Monkey year of the 16th *Rabjung* Cycle, the 2488th Buddha's parinirvana, according to the Theravada system.

8 Sept 1944
   (While in Kullu,) he wrote an article called "About the Tibetan Letters *ca* and *cha*" and "Natural transfiguration of U-chen to U-mé)".

1945
   This guidebook is an extended version of the book that he wrote twelve years after he arrived in India.

1945
   "This extended and second edition of the *Guide to the Sacred Places in India* was composed by the Amdo tourist Gendün Chöphel in the 2489th Buddha's Mahaparinirvana."

1946
   The *White Annals* (p. 32 of the Darjeeling edition):
   "This Fire-Dog year of the 16th *Rabjung* Cycle corresponds to the 2490th year of Buddha's Mahaparinirvana."

1946
Dorji Gyal:
   In the Fire-Dog year, Gendün Chöphel and Horkhang's son Sonam Pelbar surveyed the pillars at Karchung Dorji Ying Temple, Ramagang and Tashi Gephel Ling Temple at Ushangdo.

1947
Tibet Mirror, 1 January 1947
   (9th day of the 11th month of the 920th Tibetan *Rablo* Year 920), No. 3.
   "According to information received, the Tibetan government has remanded Gendün Chöphel in custody and is continuing to investigate him."

1947
   Tibet Mirror, 1 December 1951
   (2nd day of the 10th month of the 925th *Rablo* Year, Iron-Hare Year), No. 9.

"In 1947, he traveled to Tibet via South Bhutan. In the same year the Tibetan government arrested him for unknown reasons."

1949

Tibet Mirror, 1 May 1949 (923th Rablo Year, Earth-Ox Year) "Geshe Gendün Chöphel conducted study and research into many classic texts of religious history, and translated many texts of Tibetan history, as well as others from the Indian and Chinese languages during his stay in India, where he spent many years. Because of his vast knowledge, he is said to have been entrusted with the task of compiling a new Tibetan history book based on old and modern Tibetan historical texts."

1951

Tibet Mirror, 1 December 1951 (2nd day of the 10th month of the Iron-Hare Year, 925th *Rablo* Year), No.9.

"It is a matter of great sadness that the great scholar Gendün Chöphel, who had mastered both the inner and outer fields of studies, succumbed to his illness on the 15th day of the 8th month."

GENDÜN CHÖPHEL'S WORKS

Following are Gendün Chöphel's works which I have seen, or which are cited in various sources:

TRANSLATIONS

1. དགའ་པོ་སྟོན་པས་མཛད་པའི་ཇེ་སྨྲ་གྱི་རྣམ་བཤད་རི་མོ་ཅན་ (Translated into Tibetan)
2. *Engaging in the Bodhisattva's Ways of Life* (Translated into English from Tibetan)
3. *Dhammapada* (Translated into Tibetan)
4. *Ramayana* (Translated into Tibetan)
5. Shakuntala-natakam (translated into Tibetan)
6. Bhakti Yoga, the 12th chapter of the *Bhagawad Gita* (Translated into Tibetan)
7. ལེགས་སྦྱན་དགའ་པོའི་གླུ་ (Translated into Tibetan)
8. Karma Yoga (Translated into Tibetan)
9. About Samya Tara (Translated into Tibetan)

WRITINGS

1. *The Doctrine of Mind-Only School*
2. ཤེན་ཏུ་སྟ་བའི་རིག་ལམ་རྟོ་མཚར་ཅན། It has more than 150 pages.
3. *Explanation on a Non-Buddhist Doctrine*
4. *Major Differences between Buddhist and non-Buddhist Tenets*
5. *Roadmap from Lhasa to Darjeeling*
6. *Guide to the Sacred Places in Sri Lanka*
7. *Guide to the Sacred Places in India*
8. *Guide to the Sacred Places in India,* 2nd edition, 1945
9. An unfinished version of *Guide to the Sacred Places in India*
10. *Extensive Description of the World*
11. *The Book that Bought Knowledge on the World*
12. A thick book containing detailed descriptions of Indian culture, customs, food, dresses, places, forts and stone pillars, with 125 pictures and 20 different kinds of Indian food
13. *Arts of Lovemaking,* composed in Mathura, 1938
14. 2nd version of "Advice on the Tibetan Language"
15. 3rd version of "Advice on the Tibetan Language"
16. "An Alphabetical Poem in Colloquial Language" published in the *Tibet Mirror*
17. An alphabetical poem presented to Babu Tharchin
18. A song composed in Calcutta
19. A personal advice to his host Dolma Yangzom
20. "About the Lion"
21. "Precious Stone Keteka"
22. "Water and Tree"
23. "About the Flower Campaka"
24. "About the Flower Udumwara"
25. *The White Annals*
26. An article titled "བོད་ཀྱི་རྒྱལ་རབས་གསལ་བྱེད་", published in the *Tibet Mirror*
27. "ལྷས་དང་རས་ས་," appeared in the Tibet Mirror
28. An article titled "རྒྱ་བོད་མནའ་བསྒྲལ་ཚུལ་དང་། གོང་མའི་རྒྱལ་ས་བོད་ཀྱིས་བཟུང་ཚུལ་"
29. "རྒྱ་མཚོང་ནས་སྟོན་མེད་པའི་བློ་བསྐྱེད། བོད་ཡིག་བྱུང་ཚུལ་}" (Unprecedented Confidence Developed in Me after I Saw India), published in the *Tibet Mirror*

30. "About the Tibetan letters ca and cha"
31. "Natural transfiguration of U-chen to U-me"

A LIST OF RECENTLY DISCOVERED WRITINGS AND TRANSLATIONS BY GENDÜN CHÖPHEL

32. ཁྱི་བོ་ལྷང་བཙན་པོ་སྲིད་ཞི་རས་ཐང་གི་སྤྲུལ་ན་བཞུགས་དུས། (gifted to Horkhang Sonam Pelbar)
33. About a Snowy Mountain
34. Three Inherent Faults
35. ཧྲང་ཀྲུང་ལ་དཔྱད་པ།
36. A Quote Collection with Seven Characteristics
37. Petition from Dhitsa Kampo
38. Melodious Prayer for Longevity
39. བདག་མེད་བྲིས་པ། (Anonymous article)
40. Contents of the stone pillars at Lhasa, Zhöl, Samyé and others, with my annotations
41. Some Difficult Points in the texts of Madhyamika and Pramana
42. Analysis on Formations
43. A Note on Phonology
44. Some Difficult Points in Tibetan Poetry
45. Collection of Notes on Tibetan Grammar
46. ཤིན་ཏུ་སྐྱ་བའི་རིགས་ལམ་རོ་མཚར་ཅན།
47. Anthology of Sanskrit Verses
48. Tibetan history found in the 122nd chapter of the *Tang Annals* and 83rd chapter of Uygur history
49. King Trisong Detsen
50. Answers to Zhang Gawé Lodro's questions
51. Extensive description of the world
52. Description of Buddhist stupas and sacred places in India
53. ཕ་བའི་རྣམ་དཔྱོད་ཀྱི་སྒོ་སྟོན་པའི་ཕྱིར་བློ་ཆུང་ལ་བཞད་གད་ཙམ་སྟོང་བ།
(To amuse innocent minds in order to usher them to the gate of subtle intellect)
54. བཙོན་ནས་བཙན་པོ་ཁྲི་གཧུག་ལྡེ་བཙན་གྱི་མགུར་ཆིག་སྐྱད་གསར་བཅད་དུ་བཅོས་པ།
A poem composed in prison, "King Trisong Detsen's Edict on Revision of Buddhist Terminology"

Introduction 21

55. An alphabetical poem sent to Babu Tharchin
56. The Spherical World
57. An article titled "སློན་པ་མ་ནི་བུ་བའི་ལོ་རྒྱུས"⁹
58. A poem titled རྒྱམ་དབྱོད་ཆེ་ལ་སེམས་དྲང་པོའི་རིག་པའི་སྒྲེང་མོལ།
59. A poem starting with the line སློན་ཆེ་གི་ལ་ཤ་ཡི་ལོ་བྲང་དུ།
60. "བོ་ཉིད་དགའ་འདངས་པའི་ཡུན་ཚད་དུ།" A poem sent to Labrang Monastery
61. A poem composed by him at 25; the poem begins with the line "སྐྱིད་རྟེའི་བདག་ཉིད་ཤུག་ན་མརློ་དང་།"
62. A poem composed in Bangladesh, titled " མི་རྟག་དྲན་མགུར་" (Song of Impermanence) The begins with the line "རྒྱ་ཚེན་དོན་གཉིས་གྲུབ་པའི་དགའ་སློན་ལ་རོལ་པའི།"
63. A letter to his mother (dated 30 February)
64. A verse he used to recite often "རྗེས་གྲུབ་པའི་དབང་ཕྱུག་ཊི་ལི་པུ་པའི།།"
65. A rejoinder to Geshe Tsöndü; it begins with the line "ཁྱེད་དགའ་ཞམས་འགྱུར་རྟོགས་པའི་བླ།"
66. A poem sent to Geshe Chagyé Tsang, which begins with the line "སློན་ཆེ་ཨུཧྥལ་མདོག་ཅན་མའི།"
67. ཚན་རིག་གི་རང་བཞིན་ཕུན་པའི་གསར་བྱུང་གི་དངོས་པོ་མི་ཤུང་པ་མཐོང་བས་རྒྱན་བྱས་ཏེ་བླ་བྲང་དགོ་བཞིས་རྒྱམ་པར་གསར་བྱུང་གི་དངོས་པོའི་རོ་སློང་པའི་ཚུལ་དུ་ཕུལ་པའི་སྐུན་ཚོགས། "སློམ་བྱུར་བརྒྱད་འཁོར་ལོ་ཆུང་དུ་ཞིག"
    A poem titled "An eight cornered box with a small wheel" sent to the geshes of Labrang Monastery to introduce some products of modern science.
68. A letter to his mother and relatives sent in the beginning of the 5th Tibetan month, saying "It has been more than a year since I arrived in Sri Lanka..."
69. *Life of the Buddha*. This is an article sent to Geshe Gendün Gyatso of Labrang Monastery. With the first part of the text missing, it begins with the line: "...བཅབས་ཏེ་སྒྲས་པར། དེ་མ་ཐག་ཐྱོགས་བཞིར་གོམ་བདུན་བདུན་བོར་ཏེ་ཤར་ལ་གཟིགས།"
70. Articles on Buddha's pacification of six heretics, a short life history of King Ashoka according to Indian texts and King Bimbisara of Rajagriha
71. Praise to Tara, starting with the line "དུས་གསུམ་རྒྱལ་བ་ཀུན་གྱི་འཕྲིན་ལས་གཟུགས།།"
72. An alphabetic poem written when he visited the Jokhang Temple, and the poem begins with the lines "ཀ་གང་ལྟ་བར་བུ་ཞིག་སྐྲ། ཁམས་གཏང་སྱས་ཀྱི་འབས་སུ་མི་འདུག"

73. Poems including "གུན་བཟང་འཁོར་ལོ" which begins with the line "སྐུ་གསུམ་རྒྱལ་བའི་ཡེ་ཤེས་དངས་མའི་ཁམས།" sent to Minling Trichen Rinpoche
74. An article titled "ང་རྒྱལ་གྱི་ཚད་སྦྱར་བའི་ཚུལ་" (How to incite arrogance in others)
75. རྒྱལ་ཁམས་རིག་པས་བསྐོར་བའི་གཏམ་རྒྱུད་གསེར་གྱི་ཐང་མ།
    An extensive travelogue he wrote during his tour in Tibet, India and Ceylon
76. རྒྱའི་ལོ་རྒྱུས་ལས་བྱུང་བའི་བོད་ཀྱི་རྒྱལ་རབས་སྙོར།
    Tibetan history found in the Chinese annals
77. དགེ་འདུན་ཆོས་འཕེལ་གྱིས་བསྒྱུར་གནང་བའི་ཚུན་དོད་ཡིག་ཆ། ཀ། ཁ། ག།
78. དེབ་དཀར་དུ་འཁོད་པ་དང་མ་འཁོད་པའི་ཚིགས་སུ་བཅད་པ་དང་། ལོ་ཚིགས་རེ་འགའི་གནད་དོན་ལ་སྦྱར་པ།
    (16)

AUTHOR'S NOTES

i. That these charges were sent to Tibet Mirror for publication has been explained in his piece, which has lines beginning with twin-phrases like "གལ་ཆེ་གལ་ཆེ། ཡ་མཚན་ཡ་མཚན། བཤད་དཔྱད་བཤག་དཔྱད། མགྱོགས་པོ་མགྱོགས་པོ།"

ii. From the "ca cha'i skor" written in Kullu.

iii. After he joined Dhitsa Tashi Chöding Monastery, he was called Dhitsa. "Alak" means lama in Amdo language. He was also called Dhitsa Kampo, or Thin Dhitsa, because he was thin.

iv. The great scholar Jigmé Samten Rinpoche and his spiritual son named him Dodrak Tülku. He was held to be the reincarnation of a lama of Dorji Drak Nyingma Monastery.

v. The *White Annals,* stanza 4 of the homage verses.

vi. རྒྱ་གར་གྱི་གནས་ཡིག, written in 1945. See concluding portion.

vii. As recollected by Alak Jigmé Rinpoche.

viii. *Criticism to An Ornament to Nagarjuna's Intent,* p. 6.
"དེར་བཞུགས་རིག་པ་སྨྲ་བ་ཡོངས་ཀྱི་ཕ་སྐད་པ་ཞེས་སྨྲོད་པའི་ང་རོ་རྒྱ་ཆེར་བསྒྲགས་པར་བརྟེན་དབུས་ཕྱོགས་སུ་ཡོང་།" (He came to Central Tibet because scholars there strongly criticized him as non-religious."

ix. A letter to Rahul, dated 15 December 1935.

x. Y.M.B.A. School, Bhutia Busti, Darjeeling. Also called Buddhist Home in the Himalayas, Bhutia Busti, Darjeeling.

xi. Kachen Lhakdor, who had resided with Gechö at one time, told me that Gechö studied English for six months and obtained a matric (matriculation) certificate, and the news about this appeared in some newspapers. In those days, one could give matric exams even without formal qualifications.

xii. *The White Annals*
xiii. Letter from Rahul, 14 January 1936.
xiv. Letter to Rahul, undated.
xv. A letter to Rahul, dated 19 February 1936.
xvi. Communist husband of Draya Dolma Yangzom, Russian scholar Roerich and Rahula, who was also believed to be a communist.
xvii. From Prof. Samdong Rinpoche.
xviii. Some of his accounts mention a sketch of a map of Bhutan, while others mention a map of Mön Tawang, but it is certain that he made a map.
xix. *Tibet Mirror,* 1/11/1951 (2nd day of the 10th month of the Iron-Hare year, 925th *Rablo* year), Vol. 9.

"In 1947, he journeyed to Tibet via Bhutan. In the same year he was arrested by the Tibetan government for unknown reasons?"

Criticism to An Ornament to Nagarjuna's Intent, p. 6

"He always engages in bad deeds; he was even imprisoned as a punishment for a breach of the law of the state."

xx. *Tibet Mirror,* December 12, 1951.

"Last year as soon as he was released from prison, the Tibetan government requested him to compose a Tibetan history, and he accordingly started working."

xxi. *Criticism to An Ornament to Nagarjuna's Intent,* p. 6

"He traveled to foreign countries. The result was that he lost faith in the Three Precious Jewels and discarded his monastic vows in the same manner that he would discard a toilet pebble. He took pleasure in the company of women. He always engaged in bad deeds, and he even breached the law of the state so that he was imprisoned. He had such courage to do bad things. That he always drank alcohol and behaved insanely and callously was witnessed by everyone."

xxii. *Tibet Mirror,* December 1, 1951, No. 9
xxiii. In his forward to Rakra Tülku Thupten Chödar's *The Life of Gendün Chöphel,* the Dalai Lama says:

"Domépa Gendün Chöphel can be considered as one of the most progressive amongst Tibetans in the 20th century, on account of his exceptional intellect and ability to have far sighted views on all specific and general issues with due consideration to their future consequences."

xxiv. *Criticism to An Ornament to Nagarjuna's Intent,* p. 6
Gechö (Gendün Chöphel) is a psychotic, who attempts to cover with his hands the sun-like tradition of the great Jamgön Tsongkhapa. Further at page 7, "The psychotic Gendün Chöphel, who has an enormous ability to make erroneous statements…"

xxv. A draft of a news report on the arrest of Gendün Chöphel, "Bearing in mind the prophecies made by the previous Dalai Lama in the Water-Monkey year, the one who has vowed to introduce communism in Tibet is a disciple of the barbarian Rahul." It also read, "The main figure who has vowed to spread Russian communism in Tibet is Gechö."

xxvi. As explained by Gelong Rinzin Wangpo, a close friend of Tharchin, on how he dissuaded him from the preparation of a charge sheet against Gendün Chöphel.

xxvii. Preface by the XIV Dalai Lama to Rakra Tülku Thupten Chödar's *Biography of Gendün Chöphel*
"…can be considered as one of the most advanced Tibetans in the 20th century, on account of his exceptional intellect and far sighted views on all specific and general issues with due consideration to their future consequences."

Translator's Notes

1. Pomba Rabga was a son of rich Khampa bussinessman family Pomdatsang.
2. He was the favoured attendant of the Thirteenth Dalai Lama. After the Dalai Lama passed away, he was banished from Lhasa by some senior government's officials, on charges of not providing timely medical treatment to the Dalai Lama and not informing the government about the Dalai Lama's illness.

3. Changlochen Sonam Gyalpo was formerly a member of Lungshar's party called Kyichok Kunthun "Welfare Association." When Lungshar was arrested and sentenced, Changlochen, with other associates of Lungshar, was banished.
4. The female offspring of a yak and a cow or an ox and a she-yak.
5. *Damaru* is a small drum used as a ritual instrument. Here it means that Kashöpa was double-faced.
6. The Tibetan expression *"thug pa dkrug dkrug dkrugs"* means to create a controversy or to spread a rumour here and there.
7. Full Tibetan title: རྒྱལ་ཁམས་རིག་པས་བསྐོར་བའི་གཏམ་རྒྱུད་གསེར་གྱི་ཐང་མ།
8. Rablo (རབ་ལོ་) is counted from the first Rabjung year, which corresponds to 1027 AD. The present Rablo year is 985.
9. Prophet Mani (c. 216–276 AD) was the founder of Manichaeism, which is a synthesis of Christianity, Zoroastrianism and Buddhism.

What I Remember about Gendün Chöphel

Dzongu Nakdo[*]

Gendün Chöphel was born at Shopong Nyinta *(zho phong nyin lta)* [in Amdo]. Nyinta is the name of his village. His mother's name was Ama Lhamak *(a ma lha dmag)*. I do not know whether his father was a Tantric practitioner.

His mother sometimes behaved as if she was possessed by a supernatural power. It was said that she would appear to be dead for two or three days and then suddenly wake up, as if she had come back to life. I heard that her predictions were usually accurate when she performed divinations. I am not sure if she was possessed by a deity, but she must have been possessed by at least a minor deity. She could attend meetings of the deities, like the Eight Classes of Gods and Spirits *(sde brgyad)*. When she disappeared for a day or two, she might have gone to attend a meeting. I heard that she told people where she attended the meetings and how much grain, wood, hay and merchandise were demanded by the local spirits. Once she told how the deities ate up a whole dzomo she had brought in response to their demands.

Gendün Chöphel first studied under Geteng Lobzang *(sges sting blo bzang)* at a hermitage called Yama Tashikhyil *(ya ma bkra shis 'khyil)*

---

[*] He was born in a village called Dzongu *(rdzong ngu)* in Domé. During the early part of his life, he became a member of the gang of notorious robber called Gojukser *(mgo mjug ser)*, "yellow from head to feet," and was involved in a number of robberies in Domé. Later he went to Lhasa and joined the Chushi Gangdruk, a voluntary military organization based in Lhoka. In 1959 he went into exile in India and settled in Darjeeling, where he ran a small restaurant in a small place called Khé. Since he was from Gendün Chöphel's native region, he knew much about Gendün Chöphel's life history.

in Seksing *(sregs shing)*. He stayed there and gained good knowledge of the scriptures. His mother had told him that he should first become a monk and study under Geteng Lobzang, and then establish a spiritual bond with Geshe Sherab *(dge bshes shes rab tshang)*[1] of Dobi. Accordingly, after that he formed a spiritual connection with Geshe Sherab. Following this, he joined Dhitsa Monastery, where he studied the scriptures for a few years. Then he joined Labrang [Tashikhyil] Monastery, where he pursued monastic studies for several years. There he contrived a paper boat, which when filled with lamp fuel, flew across a river. This event ended badly for him. Jamyang Zhepa *('jam dbyangs bzhad pa)*[2] reprimanded him:

> nga stong phrag gsum gyi nang la//
> sdud nag can la lnga brgya yod//
> khyod rang gis de 'dra mi shes pa rtsa ba nas med//
> khyod 'dir bsdad mi chog//
>
> (Amongst three thousand people like me,
> There are five hundred malicious demons;
> It is impossible that you are not aware of this,
> You are not allowed to stay here.)

As a result, he went to Lhasa. While he was studying at Dhitsa Monastery, he was known as "Alak Dhitsa *(a lag dhi tsha)*." Alak in Amdo dialect means a tülku or a reincarnate lama.

His father was a Tantric practitioner of the Nyingma tradition, and he died when Gendün Chöphel was small. Gendün Chöphel was said to be the only child in his family.

Later, the relationship between Gendün Chöphel and Geshe Sherab became slightly strained. It might have been because Geshe Sherab came to know that he had previously been a disciple of Geteng Lobzang, and started to dislike him. They got into an argument during which Gendün Chöphel objected to his teacher's views. Angered, Geshe Sherab reprimanded him and expelled him from the room, yelling "If you don't think your teacher is right, why have you come here to study? You beggar, get out!" Gendün Chöphel retorted, "You know what I know, and I know what you know! But you know nothing more than what I know. So there is no reason for us to be teacher and disciple. You are a great man; you attend important world conferences. But I caution you to respond carefully if the modern scientists ask you questions about the formation of the universe. I don't think the so-called "four continents" and "sub-continents exist".[3] If that is what you tell others, you will eventually be disgraced."

NOTES

1. Geshe Sherab Gyatso (1884–1968) was a religious teacher at Drepung Monastery. After the death of the XIII Dalai Lama he fell from favour with the Tibetan government and returned to his home in Amdo, an eastern Tibetan area. He associated himself first with the Nationalist Government of China and then with the Communist People's Republic of China. He held a number of government posts in Tibetan areas under the People's Republic of China. He was also initially the vice-president and later the president of the Buddhist Association of China; the latter position he held until 1966. In 1968, during the Cultural Revolution, Sherab Gyatso's left leg was broken by a Red Guard. In Nov. 1st, 1968, he died. After the Gang of Four arrested, in Aug. 26th, 1978, the Qinghai government rehabilitated him.
2. Jamyang Zhepa was the head of Labrang Tashikhyil Monastery. The first Jamyang Zhepa, Kunkhen Jamyang Zhepa Dorji, founded the monastery.
3. According to the Buddhist cosmology, there are four continents and each continents has two sub-continents.

My Brief Meeting with Gendün Chöpel

*Kazi Lhündup Dorji**

Gendün Chöpel was an erudite man with a unique personality. It was rare to find him reading scriptures and doing religious practices. He had no property or belongings. He used to spend most of his time playing with small children. Sometimes, he would stay at home naked.

When he went to India, he crossed the Lachen valley in Sikkim. There, he met one of the relatives of Rinak Yapa Tseten Tashi *(ri nag ya pa tshe brtan bkra shis)*. At that time Kazi monk Jonoras[1] was looking for a Tibetan teacher to teach at the school he had recently founded in Darjeeling. He requested Gendün Chöpel to teach there. Gendün Chopel accepted the request and taught there. During the time he learned English from Jonoras.

Around that time, the Thirteenth Dalai Lama sent a letter to a Bhutanese official Drashö Raja Dorji *(drag shos ra' dza rdo rje)*[2] asking him to make an English translation of a text by Jé Tsongkhapa. Raja Dorji sought Gendün Chöpel's help, and they jointly completed the translation in two months. After that, with the help of Raja Dorji,

---

* As a son of an aristocratic family, Kazi Lhundup Dorjee became Chief Minister of Sikkim. He had a French wife, who was a close friend of Chou Enlai. She met Chou in France when they were young. Kazi's younger brother Jonaras, a Theravadin monk and a highly-educated scholar, was close to Gendün Chöpel. He might have taught English to Gendün Chöpel. He and Gendün Chöpel jointly translated the Guide to Bodhisattva's Way of Life (spyod 'jug chen mo) into English. When I went to Darjeeling in 1979 in search of information on Gendün Chöpel, I found the text of the English translation along with several other documents and papers among a corpus of Gendün Chöpel in the Tibetan village called Bhutia Busti.

Gendün Chöphel made a pilgrimage to various sacred places of Bhutan. He made a map of these sacred places in order to write a guide to the sacred places in Bhutan. This roused suspicion among some people. I heard that [Bhutanese King] Jigmé Dorji's wife[3], who was a daughter of the Tsarong family, and others sent letters to the Tibetan government complaining about Gendün Chöphel's activities. I heard that later when clarification was provided by Changlochen *(lcang lo can)*[4] and others, he was released from prison. He had already become mentally ill when he was released. I, Kazi Lhündup *(ka ji lhun grub)*[5], once suggested to him that it would be of immense benefit if he imparted his knowledge to others. In response, he said, "I can do it if there are people interested in learning. Otherwise, what am I to do?" Many scholars of his time said that if he did research and wrote books, they would have been most remarkable.

Notes

1. He was a brother of Bhutanese queen Ashi Kesang.
2. I was not able to find his correct name.
3. Ashi Kesang Choden Wangchuk, queen of the third Bhutanese King Jigmé Dorji.
4. Changlochen Sonam Gyalpo, was an associate of Pomda Rabga, a Tibetan fugitive who founded a party called Tibet Improvement Party (*nub bod legs bcos skyid sdug*) in Sikkim.
5. Kazi Lhundup Dorjee (1904-2007) was the first chief minister of Sikkim from 1974 to 1979 after its union with India. He was popularly known as Kazi Saab in Sikkim.

A Short Narration about Gendün Chöphel

Gelong Rigzin Wangpo

Gendün Chöphel was born in Domé, and he was very famous. He was very knowledgeable in every field of learning, including the traditional Tibetan fields of learning and science. He had a great talent especially in the arts of drawing and painting.

When the Indian monk Pandit Rahul [Sankrityayan][1] visited Tibet for religious study, Gendün Chöphel was at Chusinshar *(chu srin shar)*. There he became friend with Sokpo Chödrak *(sog po chos grags)*. Pandit Rahul met Gendün Chophel and Sokpo Chödrak at Chusinshar and the three became friends. When Pandit Rahul returned to India, Gendün Chöphel went with him. Sokpo Chödrak had not yet completed his Geshe exam at that time. They went to Zhalu Monastery, where they discovered many Indian Buddhist texts brought from India by Zhalu Lotsawa. Comparing the Tibetan translations with the Indian texts, Rahul was greatly impressed and praised the accuracy of the translations. They also found several ancient Indian Buddhist texts written on palm leaves. Since the manuscripts were sacred and the main object of worship for the monastery, Rahul was allowed to take with him only a few leaflets, in order to show them in India. Gendün Chöphel and Rahul then headed to Sakya where they stayed for some time. Sokpo Chödrak was not with them. At Sakya, Rahul acquired

---

* He was born into a family whose paternal root trace back to a Korean man, who arrived and settled in Lhasa long ago. He came to India and worked as the editor for Tibetan newspaper The Tibet Mirror (yul phyogs so so'i gsar 'gyur me long) in Kalimpong for many years. During that time, he and Gendün Chöphel acquainted each other and became close friends for many years. Late in his life, he became a Theravadin monk and wore the yellow robes.

several texts of Indian origin. All the texts he brought from Tibet are currently in the Patna Museum in India.

From India, Gendün Chöphel traveled to Sri Lanka and composed the *Guide to the Sacred Places in Sri Lanka*. However, that text is not available in its complete form. I think Tharchin Babu *(mthar phyin bha bu)* had a part of the text.

Gendün Chöphel translated the Pali text *Dhammapada* into Tibetan, with the title *chos kyi tshigs su bcad pa*. In our tradition, this text comes under the category of *lung phran tsheg* (Minor Precepts), the classification of minor teachings of Vinaya. He also translated several chapters of *The Bhagavad Gita*, the main text attributed to Lord Krishna, which is called *legs ldan nag po'i glu* in Tibetan. The translated chapters include "Bhakti Yoga" (Path of Devotion) and "Karma-Vairagya Yoga" (Action and Renunciation) whose Tibetan titles are *dad pa'i rnal 'byor* and *las kyi rnal 'byor*. The Ramakrishna Mission[2] based in West Bengal published the translations in Tibetan *u-chen* script. I read these two chapters.

I have heard that Gendün Chöphel also translated the entire text of *Shakuntala*, a play that falls into the same genre as the Tibetan opera Zukyi Nyima *(gzugs kyi nyi ma)*. His translations also include *The Arts of Lovemaking ('dod pa'i bstan bcos)* which was translated from Hindi and is available these days in book form. These are his works that I have seen, but I think there are many others.

Gendün Chöphel's *White Annals* is authentic and very accurate. About fifty years ago, some French explorers travelled from China to Xinjiang on an archaeological survey. During their survey, they heard a faint sound from a corner of a rock. It was the sound of fluttering paper. Greatly curious, they examined the wall and found many rolls of paper bearing texts written in (ancient) Tibetan script on one side. They pulled out as many of the scrolls as possible and took them to France. They made facsimiles of the documents and sent Bacot[3] with the texts to study them and to consult Tharchin Babu at Kalimpong about them. They sought help from Gendün Chöphel, who at that time was working as a teacher at a Christian school in Kalimpong. Tharchin Babu, Gendün Chöphel and Bacot together studied the scrolls and realised that the contents were about early Tibetan history. The texts were either fully or partially illegible. Studying the texts by comparing the contexts and the semantics of the preceding and following lines, Gendün Chöphel was able to restore the texts, almost entirely, by means of logical inference. They translated the texts and made copies of the translation. Bacot was very pleased with this work. He gave the copies to Tharchin Babu. Gendün Chöphel told them that he would copy the texts, saying that they were very valuable and would be lost if they were kept in the original form. These manuscripts became the foundation of his *White Annals*. The *White Annals* in its initial stage ran to about sixty or seventy pages. Except for the opening homage and epilogue found in the present-day *White Annals*, the main body of the text is the same.

Gendün Chöphel worked at Tharchin Babu's press from 1935 to 1941/42. He travelled everywhere in India. He also went to Sri Lanka, accompanied by Rahul. I think in Sri Lanka he learned the Pali language on a scholarship provided by the Mahabodhi Society[4] in India. At that time he knew some English. Some people have claimed that he studied English in six months and passed the matriculation exam. If that is the case, he should have been able to speak English quite fluently, but I did not hear him speaking English that well. He also knew Hindi. His proficiency in Sanskrit and Pali was great; he could make translations in both these languages. He once told me that he wanted to visit Japan and America, but he did not travel to other foreign countries (apart from India, Sri Lanka and Bhutan).

Later, he returned to Tibet and stayed at Wangden Pelbar House near Darpoling *(dar po gling)* temple in Lhasa. One day I went to see him. He was having a discussion on Nagarjuna's view of the Middle-Way (Madhyamika) philosophy with Geshe Chödrak. He said that Nagarjuna's explanation on *Madhyamika* was exaggerated, and then he gave a short explanation of the philosophy and said "this much is sufficient". I didn't have much knowledge of Buddhist philosophy, but I felt doubtful about his statements and did not like his words.

Later, I thought of studying a non-Tibetan subject with him, but he was soon arrested and imprisoned. Different rumours about his arrest circulated at that time. Some said that he was arrested for possession of counterfeit Tibetan 100-rupee notes, while others said that he was charged with planning to introduce Bolshevism into Tibet. Although we were close friends, I dared not visit him in prison, fearing that it might bring me unwelcome problems. Sokpo Geshe Chödrak visited him in prison sometimes. When he was released, I was already in India. Some people told me that he had returned from India after he and Pandit Rahul had made a plan to spread communism in Tibet. I didn't know what the truth was.

Rahul had been to the USSR[5] and had a Russian wife. Later he travelled to Tibet and spent some time in Sakya, during which he lived with a daughter of Jango *(byang sgo)*, a wealthy man and close attendant of the Sakya Lama. After he returned to India, the woman gave birth to a girl, who had an Indian look. People called the child Ratruk *(ra phrug)*. When I heard the name "Ratruk" for the first time, I thought it meant "baby goat" because 'ra phrug' in Tibetan means "goat's child". But later I came to know that it meant "Rahul's child". She later arrived in India.

While in India Gendün Chöphel became very close to Pomda Rabga *(spom mda' rab dga')* and his party. Their main goal was to introduce democracy (in Tibet). However, they could not achieve their aim as their secret plans leaked out. I was young at that time. They had also published a booklet explaining the aims and objectives of their group. I think Rabga wanted to make Kham an independent state, and to seek support from the Kuomintang government if the Tibetan government sent armed forces to Kham. The party was said to have a logo, but I have not seen it. The logo was designed by Sokpo Dharma *(sog po dhar ma)* in great secrecy. When their activities became public, there were rumours about Sokpo Dharma forging (Tibetan) 100-rupee currency notes. The British government of India raided the houses of Rabga, Kuchar Kunphel *(sku bcar kun 'phel)*[6], Changlochen *(lcang lo can)* and Sokpo Dharma, and burned all their documents and seals, among other things. Babu Tharchin was also suspected of being involved, but they could not search his house as he worked for the Indian government. Sensing imminent trouble, Rabga fled to China via Hong Kong. His associates were each served with a very harsh reprimand. I am not sure if Gendün Chöphel received such a reprimand: he left for Tibet by way of Bhutan.

When Gendün Chöphel's house in Lhasa was raided—it was perhaps in 1944—a humorous incident occurred. As the police were ransacking the room, one constable saw something hidden under a sheet in a corner. As he lifted the sheet, he saw something that frightened him so much so that he ran out of the room and shouted to his colleagues, "There is someone inside! A woman!" It was actually a female rubber dummy.

Gendün Chöphel was put in an underground prison at Zhöl Office. The conditions inside the prison were not too bad. I think he was allowed to receive whatever was brought in from outside the jail.

As for his lifestyle, he seemed to be somewhat of a philanderer, as reflected in his work *Arts of Lovemaking*, which recounts his visit to different places (brothels). Later, when he was residing at Jamyang Kyil, he was living with a woman from Kham. He drank and smoked excessively, and wore only a white sheet all the time. At that time, he appeared somewhat unbalanced.

Kashöpa stole Gendün Chöphel's manuscript of the *Book that Bought Knowledge of the World ('dzam gling shes bya nyos pa'i deb)* which was said to contain notes on various topics of history, politics and so forth. It was in fact his personal diary. When he was arrested, all his books, manuscripts and notes were seized, and a committee was set up to examine them. Kashöpa was suspected of having taken some of them. It was the British government of India that was responsible for his arrest. I don't think he had actually been committing any offenses—his arrest might have been due to the activities of some of the people with whom he associated.

Notes

1. Rahul Sankrityayan (1893-1963), who is called the Father of Hindi Travel literature, was one of the most widely-traveled scholars of India,

spending forty-five years of his life on travels away from his home. He became a Buddhist monk (Bauddha Bhikkhu) and eventually took up Marxist Socialism. He is referred to as the 'Greatest Scholar' (Mahapandit) for his scholarship. He was both a polymath as well as a polyglot. He visited Tibet twice to search for Indian palm-leave manuscripts. He met Gendün Chöphel and they became friends.

2. The Ramakrishna Mission is a philanthropic, volunteer organization founded by Ramakrishna's chief disciple Swami Vivekananda on May 1, 1897. The Mission conducts extensive work into health care, disaster relief, rural management, tribal welfare, elementary and higher education and culture. It uses the combined efforts of hundreds of ordered monks and thousands of householder disciples. The Mission, which has its headquarters at Belur Math in Howrah, West Bengal near Kolkata, India, subscribes to the ancient Hindu philosophy of Vedanta. It is affiliated with the monastic organization Ramakrishna Math, with whom it shares members.

3. Jacques Bacot (1877–1965) was an explorer and pioneering French Tibetologist. He travelled extensively in India, western China, and the Tibetan border regions. He was the first western scholar to study the Tibetan grammatical tradition, and along with F. W. Thomas (1867–1956) belonged to the first generation of scholars to study the Old Tibetan Dunhuang manuscripts. He had help from Gendün Chöphel when studying the Dunhuang manuscripts.

4. The Mahabodhi Society was founded by the Sri Lankan Buddhist leader Anagarika Dhammapala in May, 1891 with the aim of resuscitating Buddhism in India and restoring the ancient Buddhist shrines at Buddha Gaya, Sarnath and Kushinara. Its headquarters are in Calcutta, and its main focus has been the restoration and revival of the glory and sanctity of Buddha Gaya. The Society's first centre was at Buddha Gaya. Later centres were established in Sarnath, Sanchi, Lucknow, Orissa, New Delhi, Chennai Ajmer, Bangalore etc.

5. USSR (Union of Soviet Socialist Republic), also called the Soviet Union, was formed in 1922 after the collapse of the Russian Empire in the aftermath of the Russian Revolution in 1917. Following the Soviet's

leader Mikhail Gorbachev's introduction of liberal policies, the USSR broke down in 1991 with most of its republics becoming independent.

6. Kuchar Künphel was the Thirteenth Dalai Lama's favourite attendant. After the Dalai Lama passed away in 1933, he was accused by the Tibetan National Assembly of negligence in not giving the Kashag accurate information about the Dalai Lama's health. He was expelled to Kongpo, from where he went to India. For details, see K. Thondup, *The Water-Bird and Other Years: the History of the Thirteenth Dalai Lama and After*, New Delhi: Rangwang Publisher, 208-217.

Gendün Chöphel in My Memory

Tethong Rakra Rinpoche*

I heard Gendün Chöphel's name for the first time when I was at my monastery through his book *Guide to the Sacred Places in India*, which greatly enthralled me. He had probably left for India just before I joined the monastery (where he had stayed). At the monastery, everyone praised him for his extensive knowledge of the scriptures. Later, when I went to India on a pilgrimage, I saw his *History of Sri Lanka (sing ga la'i lo rgyus)*. It was so beautifully written that it instilled in me a strong desire to visit the country, so much so that I felt I should go there immediately. These two books filled me with admiration for him, although I was still young then.

Afterwards, when I was uncertain as to whether I should join the Mahabodhi Society, I heard that he had arrived back in Tibet. He was living at Wangden Pelbarkhang House in Lhasa and I immediately went to meet him. He was pleased to see me. I requested him to teach me grammar and poetry, but he asked me, "Have you studied the scriptures well? If you have learned the scriptures well, only then is the study of grammar and poetry worth pursuing. If not, there is no use in studying grammar and composition." Saying this, he taught me *dpag bsam 'khri shing* along with its Sanskrit text *Kalpalatavadanam*. When teaching the text, he would sometimes become over-excited and read

---

* Born in 1924 in Lhasa into an aristocratic family of Tethong, he was recognized as the reincarnation of a lama at a very young age, and was admitted to Drepung Monastery. He took Geshe Lharampa and Ngag-rampa degrees in succession. He has served Tibetan religion and culture in his various capacities and he is currently based in Switzerland. As he studied Tibetan poetry, grammar, and other traditional subjects under Gendün Chöphel, he is one of the important sources on Gendün Chöphel's life.

the text in a peculiar tone as the Indian panditas do nowadays. "By doing so, it will create an auspicious condition for further study and training," he explained. He taught me the chapters on Kashyapa (*'od srungs*), Manibhadra (*nor bzang*) and Kunaal (*khu byug*) and finally the 108th chapter of the said text. While explaining the text, he would enact each scene and portray all the moods and expressions. After that, I studied with him the middle and final sections of *The Mirror of Poetry* (*snyan ngag [me long ma]*). When I showed him poems I composed as examples, he appreciated them.

Initially I did not know about any allegations against him. Monks at my monastery advised me to keep away from him. Some people told me that he was a communist and many other negative things about him, but I did not pay any attention to their comments.

One summer's day, he came to see me, and when he talked at length about his work *White Annals*, I felt great empathy for him from the core of my heart. I found that many people disliked him and I was very worried that he would not be able to finish the book. Therefore, I told him to leave all the documents with me, saying that I would never lose them. I added that since there were many visitors coming to see him, there was a great danger of losing the manuscripts, and that it would be a terrible thing if they were lost. Finally, I advised him to bring a few pages to my house. He replied that it was impossible to do so. It would indeed have been impossible for me to compose a book, but I could have at least managed to save the manuscripts had he given them to me at that time, and he could have completed the *White Annals*.

His book *Extensive Description of the World* (*'dzam gling rgyas bshad*) was remarkable. It contained notes on a wide range of topics. In the *Story of Lion* (*seng ge'i skor*), he had described the evolution of lion, the method of drawing a lion, whether the lion in the traditional Tibetan paintings were modeled on the traditional Chinese paintings, and so forth. There was also an essay titled "Note on Stone." I borrowed all of them from him to read, and later returned them to him. I also borrowed his translation of the *Ramayana* and made copies for myself. I read the chapters "Ka", "Kha", "Ga" and "Nga", but I lost the "Nga". I also read his *History of Sri Lanka*.

One day he again came to my house. I asked him if I could borrow his *White Annals*, and he refused. He told me that he wanted to teach me a grammar text called *sgra mtshams sbyor lnga pa*, a section from a Sanskrit book on grammar and composition. I joyfully accepted his suggestion.

The next day, my servant came to me hurriedly and said, "Gendün Chöphel and another man—most likely the Sherpa of Dungtsé-zur *(gdung rtse zur)*—have been arrested and imprisoned." I asked him why they had been arrested, and he said that they were charged with counterfeiting Tibetan 100-rupee currency notes. And that was what we heard from public. However, Gendün Chöphel would never make counterfeit currency notes; I knew instantly that it was just a false accusation against him. My sister was with me at that time. We were both shocked and upset by the news, and we at once sent bedding and clothes to him.

There was an army officer's son who was very arrogant and called himself a revolutionary. He and his gang often went to the prison and taunted Gendün Chöphel. I think their behaviour upset many people. From our side, apart from sending him clothes and blankets, we could do nothing for him while he was in prison.

Rampa *(ram pa)* was a cabinet minister at that time. I approached him, while someone else from our side went to Zurkhang *(zur khang)* to secure Gendün Chöphel's release. I also went to meet Kashöpa at his residence. His son was there and we had known each other since our childhood. I told him that I wanted to meet his father. Just then the old man arrived and asked me, "What is your business?" I replied, "Gendün Chöphel has been arrested on a charge of counterfeiting currency notes. He is truly a learned scholar; he would never involve himself in politics nor would he counterfeit notes. Please release him as soon as possible." His son said, "Who is Gendün Chöphel? Who does he look like?" "Such a liar," I thought. When Gendün Chöphel completed his book *Arts of Lovemaking*, he sent the first complimentary copy to Kashöpa as an expression of gratitude for the help he had received earlier. I personally saw him send a copy of his *History of Sri Lanka* to Kashöpa. However, Kashöpa ordered his arrest at the instigation of the British and Bhutanese governments. Pomda Apo Rabga and his associates were suspected of plotting to bring revolution to Tibet. As Gendün Chöphel was good at drawing, they might have requested him to travel to Bhutan and draw a map of the country, as it was a part of Tibet. He did so. After he came here (India), they included him in their party[1]. However, though his name was in the list of its membership, it did not have his signature.

I know exactly what happened with Gendün Chöphel. The British in India disliked him, because they viewed him as a modern Tibetan who could instigate reforms in Tibet. They were very worried about it. Hence, they tried to harm him in every possible way. As a last resort, they used Kashöpa to harm him. It was bad luck for him.

The publication of *Dhammapada* was funded by my brother. Gendün Chöphel presented the first complimentary copy to Kashöpa out of great respect to him. After going through the text, Kashöpa exclaimed, "The Tantric terminology is really different!" It made Gendün Chöphel burst out laughing, because the *Dhammapada* is not a Tantric text and it cannot have tantric terms. This further provoked Kashöpa. Therefore, Kashöpa imprisoned him in Nangtseshak prison.

For about three weeks, we sent food to him through the prison guard. He sent us replies written in verses, all reflecting his mental agony. Some of his verses gave us the impression that he was a real ascetic. He wrote me many poems, in some of which he had drawn an analogy between a movie theatre and samsara, comparing the theatre screen with samara and all the different images projected on the screen as suffering and happiness.

We always feared that the government might drag us into the case as well. I requested Kyabying Lobzang Thechok *(skyabs dbyings blo bzang theg mchog)* to appeal to the authorities who had authority over Gendün Chöphel's case. One day, he came to me and said, "I think it is better to keep away from Gendün Chöphel's case—it involves a lot of politics."

I think Apo Rabga had sent a letter to the Tibetan government. The letter contained a list of the members of his party, including the name of Gendün Chöphel. This startled the government. Whatever their aims were, they were not communists. I think they were plotting a coup d'état in Tibet, although I did not know the details of the party's activities. All I know about Gendün Chöphel is this much.

At my monastery, everyone said that Gendün Chöphel possessed many documents related to communism. They even accused my brother and me of climbing a ladder, entering his room at night through the window and hiding all the documents. However, as we had committed no wrong, we did not worry and continued our correspondence with him. All of those letters later fell into the hands of the *drungtsi*[2] officials. Our letters [fortunately] contained only religious topics, such as questions and answers on a particular point in the scriptures, and nothing political.

Neushar *(sne'u shag)* and Namsé Lingpa *(rnam sras gling pa)*, I think, were on the investigating committee. Kashöpa ordered the flogging of Gendün Chöphel, saying that it was mandatory by law for criminals to receive "arrival and departure floggings."[3] Citing flogging as being legally provided by the Tibetan government, Kashöpa sternly insisted on the floggings. The investigating committee could not veto his order and gave Gendün Chöphel some fifty floggings. Gendün Chöphel later told me that the investigating committee gave him special consideration and that they whipped him only under compulsion. He further said that the punishment was nothing compared to the ones given to other people. Since he had never received such a beating since his childhood, the whip itself was more frightening than the actual pain it brought him. He was later transferred to Zhöl prison during the Great Prayer Festival. The conditions there seemed slightly relaxed. Whenever possible, I went to give food to him.

India was due to celebrate its first Independence Day and the officials of the Tibetan government were discussing what present they should offer to the Indian government on that occasion. The Regent Taktra Rinpoche decided that they should offer a scroll painting of King Ashoka and instructed that the task of making the painting should be given to Gendün Chöphel. Had they commissioned him, he surely would have created a perfect painting of King Ashoka, which would have made the people of India feel that the Tibetans had an interest in and awareness about India. However, whether or not the Tibetan government presented a painting to India during the event, I do not know.

In prison, Gendün Chöphel often received different kinds of snacks from the Regent [Taktra] and the junior tutor [of His Holiness the 14th Dalai Lama]. When the managers and monk officials of a monastery do something, the Lamas cannot stop them. Gendün Chöphel told me about this after he was released. If someone else were in his place, he would hold a grudge against the persons who imprisoned him. On the contrary, he praised them. He exclaimed with surprise, "I have never seen such a free and unbounded prison as here. In Bhutan, the prisons are very congested and very restricted. In Zhöl prison, the prisoners are free to do anything they like; there is no one who keeps an eye on them. Such a good government!"

After several days he was transferred to Zhöl prison, and I said to him, "I feel really sorry that despite trying hard, I find it difficult to seek your release." He replied in verses. The import of his reply was: "I have always been engaged in the study of the scriptures and striving for knowledge. While in India, I conducted research on Sanskrit and Pali. I did this solely with the idea that it would benefit Tibet; I didn't have any other motives. So don't be upset." Two lines in his reply read:

> A flower blossomed in a land facing north,
> But it withered away in the same land facing north.

When the Sera and Reting monks organized an armed uprising against the government (against the arrest of Reting Rinpoche)[4], Gendün Chöphel was in Zhöl prison. As a scholar, he would always view things from a positive perspective, not from a negative point of view. He told us many interesting stories about his life in prison. He once told me:

> One of my inmates was serving a life sentence. As he had stayed there for a long time, a degree of mutual trust had developed between him and the prison guard. The guard allowed him to visit his home in Phenpo for three months of summer every year. It is incredible. The guard would advise him to come back on time and to be careful, or else the higher officials would know. The prisoner would say, "Of course sir," and he used to come back at the right time.

He also recalled:

> In the prison, there were Bu Lama *(bu bla ma)* and Tsenya Trülku *(rtse nya sprul sku)* who were involved in the Reting riots. One morning somebody called us saying that an old man called Minchik *(ming gcig)* had died in his cell and we should go there to see him immediately. When we got there, I found him dead with his body in the posture of *sa gnon mnyam gzhag*, the earth-suppressing meditative posture.

He wrote many beautiful poems, including "Who can enjoy prison life so much as we Buddhists do?" When he was released, he had grown his hair to this much (shoulder-length). There was on his table a beautifully drawn image of the Goddess Tara. He was skilled in drawing and painting. He told me that he had drawn it while in prison. He said, "Whether I call her my beloved spouse or girlfriend, she is the one who gave me company and comforted me in prison." He then said, "I am just joking. I recited the praise to Goddess Tara 100,000 times in the prison." He was such a holy man.

Tsenya Rinpoche became popular, as people in Lhasa believed that he was very skilful artist. They received paintings from him, and regarded them as very sacred. Later, when I inquired, I found that the paintings were not made by him. I don't think he could draw even a good circle. Actually, he used to give the paintings made by Gendün Chöphel to others, pretending that they were his own works. The fact is that when in prison Tsenya Rinpoche used to give paintings made by Gendün Chöphel as gifts to people who came to meet him at the prison, pretending they were done by him. Later, Gendün Chöphel told us about this and he felt very bad about it.

Before his arrest, he never drank alcohol, but after his release, he started drinking excessively. The Agriculture Department of the government provided him with a salary and a house.

In prison, he had met a young girl. Whether she was his maidservant or his wife, she lived in his room.

I saw Dawa Zangpo[5], the author of the *An Ornament to Nagarjuna's Intent (klu sgrub dgongs rgyan)*, visiting Gendün Chöphel frequently. I found him a very cunning person. When he first came, Gendün

Chöphel told him to go away. I do not know why he did this. But Dawa Zangpo insisted on coming inside. People said that Dawa Zangpo behaved like Milarepa. Finally, he got an opportunity to study the scriptures with Gendün Chöphel.

Meru Ta Lama's Lobzang Phuntsok and others requested Gendün Chöphel to explain in detail his earlier statement "I don't know if they are conventionally established" which appeared in his work *An Ornament to Nagarjuna's Intent*. Gendün Chöphel showed it to me once before his arrest, and said regretfully, "I made a mistake by writing such things with my unrestraint hands." I responded, "Was it of any use to you?"

To a member of the Nyingma tradition, Gendün Chöphel was purely a Nyingma follower, because he had extensive knowledge of the Nyingma doctrines. Similarly, if a member of the Kagyü sect asked him about the Kagyü tradition, he could explain all the teachings of the Kagyü school. If you ask him about the arts of thievery and robbery, he would tell you many things about them. His knowledge was so extensive that there was nothing he did not know.

Later, he moved to Horkhang's residence. At that time, his health was very weak.

Gendün Chöphel's father was a Tantric master from Rebgong. At the time of Gendün Chöphel's birth, there were many auspicious signs. When his father died, he had visions of beautiful rainbows. He loudly cried, "Those little girls are taking my father away!" Some dakinis might have come to escort his father to the celestial realms. His father died when he was still a child.

He seems to have been very mischievous during his childhood. He once said to me:

> I encounter many adversaries, I don't know why? It may be because I created many lingas (phallic stones) in my father's meditation cave. Or it could be because I translated the *Bhagavad Gita*. During the time of Sakya Pandita, an Indian scholar Simhananda came to Tibet. Sakya Pandita defeated him and ordered the Twelve Female Protective Deities *(brtan ma bcu gnyis)* to punish severely whoever brought even a single page of non-Buddhist text, let alone a whole text, into Tibet. I have no rebellious thoughts towards the Tibetan

government. I expelled some malignant spirits from my father's meditation cave. On the other hand, I also translated the *Bhagavad Gita* and brought it to Tibet. May be this is a punishment from the Twelve Female Protective Deities of Tibet.

He told me many similar stories about himself. He looked like a real saint. At times, he recited the *Five Treatises of Maitreya (byams chos sde lnga), Ornament of Clear Realization and Supplement to Clear Realization* loudly with an Amdo tune. He was in good spirits when he did this. However, sometimes he wept without any reason. One day when I went to him, I saw his eyes were red. When I asked what had happened to him, he replied, "This morning I was not happy. I went down to the river and cried a lot, which gave me great relief."

He used to have very strange visions and experiences. He once said to me, "Amazing! Isn't it strange that I always dream about a statue of Avalokiteshvara the night before I meet a genuine reincarnate lama!" There are some stories about him that are beyond our understanding.

Just before I was appointed to be proctor *(dge bskos)* of a Tantric college, I visited Gendün Chöphel at his residence. Since he had just been released from prison, he felt upset if I did not go to see him frequently. He seemed to be thinking that I was not visiting him when he was in a miserable condition. Since I was about to become a monastic proctor, I felt awkward meeting him at that time, and I was about to assume the proctor's responsibilities. I explained to him that given my appointment to this responsible position, I might not be able to see him for another six months. He said, "This is quite true. I can see that it's not easy to be a proctor of a Tantric college. But on thinking closely about it, I would like to say that you should neither trouble the monks, nor expel any monks from the monastery, as they are devoted to the study of both Sutra and Tantra. Jé Rinpoche managed to incorporate all the four classes of Tantras within the confines of the three-piece robes. [He gestured clutching the fingers of his left hand tightly with his right hand.] You should know these. You must think that you are only to serve the dedicated practitioners. There are disciplinarians who unnecessarily mistreat monks; I think this is not permissible. The deity Dhamchen Chogyal is extremely strict and severe. One time when members of the Tantric college of Labrang Tashikhyil were conducting Homa rites at Chakhar *(lcags mkhar)*, I happened to laugh uncontrollably. This, as I was told, led to my expulsion at the command of Dhamchen Chogyal." I asked "How did it happen? He replied,

> At Labrang Tashikhyil, the Homa rites are conducted very carefully. The monks dig seven layers underground, and a painter draws a picture of a phallus on the bottom surface. When it is the time to draw the soul-syllable on the phallic image, the chief ritual master and his assistant monks wear black cloaks and tie black ribbons on their foreheads. The monk who is Vajracharya, or the master of ceremony, has a red face, and thus looks similar to a Huihui[6]. After wearing a black robe, he looks exactly like a Huihui.
>
> So at that time I burst out laughing uncontrollably. My laughter was so bad that I could not stop. It tempted other monks to laugh. There was a little confusion at that time.
>
> That night I had a weird dream, in which I was chased by a huge mad Yak that nearly crushed me between his horns. In great fear, I ran through many remote areas. Turning back, I could see the Yak still enraged and advancing. After the dream, I didn't feel like staying at Labrang. The protector deity of the monastery was firm in his speech and actions; he warned me to be careful.

I asked him how he had become so knowledgeable. He said, "There is no use explaining it"; he was not willing to tell the truth. I said, "I might know a reason behind this refusal. It may be due to a positive mental disposition acquired from your past lives or a miraculous event that has happened in this life." He replied, "Once when I was a child, I dreamed that a shower of DHI: syllables fell all over my body. From then on, whatever I read, even once, remains clear and strong in my mind." Therefore, it is absurd to call Gendün Chöphel a communist.

He toured various sacred sites and cities in India and wrote a very fine guidebook. The book records some very amazing incidents at some sacred places. He recounted how he could not hold back his tears when he saw the Arya statue at Garzha. He recollected, "When I opened my eyes after weeping there for a while, I found that the statue had released nectar and it had become wet. The liquid immediately vanished like fog leaving behind a few drops. When I tasted it, it tasted like water. Later, when I narrated this event to Kyabje [Trijang] Rinpoche, he told me that he had also had such experiences. Gods, humans and hungry ghosts perceive the same thing differently. Even if it is nectar, for us it is water."

Gendün Chöphel later told Zangpo that when he became sick, reciting *Praise to the Dependent Arising (rten 'brel bstod pa)* one time immediately cured his illness. At the time of his death, I was in Kalimpong and so could not attend him. During the last days of Gendün Chöphel, Dawa Zangpo resorted to very pitiful acts. Because he wanted to complete his own book, he used to hide bottles of liquor in his robes and sneak into Gendün Chöphel's house. Gendün Chöphel would feel refreshed after drinking, and Dawa Zangpo would then seek explanations and clarifications to his queries.

Some of us, including Horkhang Jolak and Gendün Chöphel's wife, tried hard to stop his unhealthy drinking habits. Dawa Zangpo gave liquor to him so as to pilfer information from him to write in his own book. He did this from selfish motives, not as a friendly gesture. In this way, Gendün Chöphel's ill health deteriorated. He once told me that he would remain alert at the time of his death so as to be able to get a vivid and describable experience of the entire process of dying. After his death, I received a letter from Horkhang Jolak about his death. Gendün Chöphel had requested Horkhang to recite *Praise to the Dependent Arising* with him three times. In the third round of their recitation, his breathing stopped as they came across the lines:

It is through the kindness of my master
I have met with the teaching of the unexcelled Buddha.

Gendün Chöphel was such a fine person. His patriotism and love for Tibet were exemplary. He would always playfully remark, "We nomadic and Amdo people from Golok have patriotism towards Tibet. How happy we would be if anybody acknowledged this patriotism?" He used to say such things. His talks were amazingly pleasing. Whether he spoke, whether on philosophical tenets, thieves or bandits, his narratives were all awe-inspiring.

One evening, something surprising happened. I was a monk at that time and I did not drink liquor. So my disciple served liquor to Gendün Chöphel while we both sat and had a long conversation on various topics. After a while, he stood up and walked outside. He said, "Tonight the moon is shining bright. As you have learnt poetry from me, just take a glance at the moon and compose a poem for me now. I said:

> The moon, the diadem of a mountain,
> Attracts the great swans by its charming;
> Seeing her unassuming white beams
> Gives me an inexpressible joy.

To this he said, "This is how to compose a poem. You have to look at an object and savour its taste. Since your poem is ad libitum, it lacks proper composition. But this is the way of composing a poem!"

He told me how his own teacher had taught him poetry. His teacher had taught him that he should call *chu 'dzin* (water vase) for cloud, not *sprin pa* (cloud) and *dal 'gro* (slow goer) for water, not *chu* (water). Then we came inside the house. He was quite drunk. He could not even mumble. After a while, for no reason, my own tongue became heavy and difficult to move. My disciple suspected that Gendün Chöphel had forced me to drink, and was angry with him.

A few days later, I told Gendün Chöphel about the intoxicated feeling I had had the last time we were together. He said, "That's right. On that day, I didn't have many thoughts; we talked and behaved like a teacher and a disciple. You listened to my talk, which produced an intoxicating effect on you. We Tibetans call it *gzi mda'* (intoxicating shot). Just think closely, don't we have something called the 'union of minds?' So, that was a sign of achieving what we call 'union of minds' *(thugs yid gcig tu 'dres)* and such things can be explained from the Tantric standpoint. You did not consume even a drop of liquor at that time; it was I who drank. But you were intoxicated. So you can see how it happened."

When I was about to leave Tibet, I told him that he should go to India and that it was useless for him to remain in Tibet. However, he did not listen to me. He had a strong desire to leave and did not want to stay there. He died in the same year I left Tibet. I wonder if he was fifty-two or fifty-three when he died. He must have been in his fifties at that time.

He was very polite. When his wife showed up when we were together, he would feel very uncomfortable, and would politely ask her to have a sense of decorum. Many people from all walks of life used to come to see him at his residence. Whoever came to him, he was able to converse with the person according to his or her disposition.

Regretfully, the text of his work Extensive Descriptions of the World seems to have completely disappeared, which I think is a huge loss. His *Story of a Lion* is also nowhere to be seen. He told me frankly that the image of the Tibetan snow lion was based on the Pekingese. The beautiful verses in the opening portion of the *An Ornament to the Nagarjuna's Intent* including the line "Infuriated, Lord Indra let his ballista off" were composed while he was in a state of intoxication.

Although Dawa Zangpo laid claims to many of the interludes in the text, they were all actually composed by Gendün Chöphel. I cannot say anything about their views. Dawa Zangpo claimed to have received a statue of Nagarjuna as a gift from Gendün Chöphel. It might be true. Gendün Chöphel had statues of Goddess Tara and Lord Buddha. He told me that the image of the Buddha was his "inseparable possession." He added, "At times when I set out on pilgrimages to the sacred places in India, sometimes I had no place to stay and was without help. During those days, this was my only reliable friend." He did not even have an amulet to put it in. He used to carry the statue in his hands. He had composed a song during his stay in Calcutta.

I think Gendün Chöphel was in his early twenties when he first arrived in Lhasa. He was born in Rebkong in the Amdo region of Tibet. He was also known as Dhitsa Alak. He acted as *dobdob* at a monastery for some time. His knowledge of the scriptures was remarkable. He and Ven. Ngawang Nyima were classmates, and whenever there were inter-collegiate debates, their class was the centre of attention. Lubum Geshe Sherab Gyatso used to say that Gendün Chöphel was his disciple, while Gendün Chöphel said he was not. Geshe Sherab behaved as if Gendün Chöphel was his disciple. I believed in him and did not say anything. In those days, Geshe Sherab seemed a bit cross with Phabongka Rinpoche, as he always gave teachings on *Stages of Path (lam rim)* and others, many monk students attended the teachings, instead of studying their monastic courses. It was said that whenever monks of Lubum monastic section attended the Rinpoche's teachings, Geshe Sherab would give each of them a hundred floggings on their return. He would say that Gendün Chöphel's case was an exception and that he was not his disciple.

Gendün Chöphel had deep faith and respect for Phabongka. He reminisced how during his visits, Phabongka would slip his hands through the collar into his back and affectionately say, "These students could be infested by lice," and then would lightly rub his back.

During one particular debate, he defeated the opponent class, whose students were mostly Mongolians. In debates, there was a certain dialectical approach to understanding the myriad phenomena "Whether all objects of knowledge are flat." When he was confronted with this question, he playfully quipped, "It is not mandatory for all objects of knowledge to be flat, but all Mongolians have flat heads." After the debates, Geshe Sherab Gyatso would invite him to his place and ask him to sleep. He would say, "Today you relax" and would serve him momos, may be as a reward for his performance in the debates.

Later, Geshe Sherab was invited to China. Before he left for China, he boasted to Gendün Chöphel, "Gendün Chöphel, you see. This time I will prove to the scholars by means of debate that the earth is flat. I will quote *mdo sde dran pa nyer bzhag* (Sutra of Mindfulness) and the third chapter of *mngon pa mdzod* (Abhidharmakosha) and prove this to them." To this Gendün Chöphel remarked, "That's good. If they respond to your hypothetical statements, it is very good. But if, instead of challenging your position, you see the foreign scholars laughing behind their hands, you'll be really embarrassed." From that time, Geshe Sherab and Gendün Chöphel did not get along.

Geshe Sherab had told Chöphel many interesting stories about his past lives. He told him about how a being from the human *bardo* state (intermediate stage between death and birth) assumed the body of an animal. According to him, he was a woman once in a previous life; she died suddenly while digging in her field. After death, in the Bardo state, she took the form of a family's ox. Later when he was reborn as Geshe Sherab, he was able to recognize the family from his former life. Chöphel recalled how they would talk a lot about such topics.

Chöphel had several paintings that he had done in Sri Lanka. He later offered them to Jamyang Zhepa, whom he revered very deeply.

Once, my brother said to Chöphel, "You are a great scholar. Instead of draping yourself in such frayed clothes, why don't you wear monk's robes?" He replied, "If I dress in monk's robes, I would certainly make a pleasing image, but I can never deceive the Buddha. I will never mislead the people, and the Buddha in particular, by feigning to be a monk or a Tantric practitioner." So until his last breath, he dressed himself in threadbare, ragged clothes. He always wore a *chupa* in an Amdo style, with the folds and plaits rolled up at the waist, giving the wearer an unkempt look.

He first went to India via Kalimpong. He seemed to have lived in Kullu (nowadays in Himachal Pradesh) for a long time. But it was in Sikkim that he studied English. In Sikkim, he had a sponsor, who helped him for a long time. After having learnt how to write quite well in English, he did not read any books. Instead, he read a dictionary all the time. His way of studying was very different. Once he had a private philosophical discussion about mental attitude and happiness and suffering with someone, probably a foreigner, and explained about these things in terms of a weighing scale and a weight. He told me about this, but I do not remember the details now.

Gendün Chöphel had thoroughly studied the section on dreams from the nine-fold unifications of the *Six Doctrines of Naropa*. He claimed to have gained control over his dreams. He once said, "If I decide that today I will retrieve my dreams, when I wake up, I continue to see the things like elephants and horses that I see in my dreams. They fade when someone wakes me up from that state. Even after consciously seeing dreams as dreams, when I compare things like paper, I do not see any difference between a real piece of paper and paper that I see in my dreams."

He was indeed a great saint-scholar. He went to Kullu and later helped [George] Roerich, a prominent Russian artist, in translating the entire *Blue Annals (deb ther sngon po)*. Although Roerich took the credit for this, the entire work was undertaken by Gendün Chöphel. It seems that Chöphel composed his song at that time. Later at Calcutta railway station, he met Roerich who was accompanied by his mother. Roerich's mother was unusually stingy. Roerich first gave him only one hundred rupees, but when his mother was out of sight, he came back and gave him a gold coin. Gendün Chöphel faced great difficulties throughout this entire venture.

He also traveled to South India to conduct research on the four forms of Tantric initiations conducted by the *siddhas* (accomplished practioners), and particularly on the means of bestowing the third initiation *(dngos dbang)*. He composed an illustrated explanation on the Evam by Krishnacharya, one of the 80 Indian mahasiddhas. It was mostly on Samvara Tantra. He also wrote other books and articles including *Guide to the Sacred Places in Sri Lanka, Extensive Descriptions of the World, Story of a Lion, Ramayana, Guide to the Sacred Places in India, Arts of Lovemaking* and several poems. If you read *Guide to the Sacred Places in Sri Lanka*, it will instantly inspire you to tour the place right away. It also contains several beautiful verses, which I don't remember now. The verses were written in a modern poetic style.

He also wrote articles on important festivals and monastic ethics, discussing the behaviour of fully ordained monks. His fields of interest included even the smallest of creatures such as insects.

His description of the Karmic law of causality is really funny. He said, "In Sri Lanka, there is an insect called a [dung] beetle, which we Tibetans call *bu zidira ('bu zi ldir ra)*. One beetle rolls mud into a small ball, while another one carries it on its back. With one carrying or pulling from the front and the other pushing from behind, they carry it." Gendün Chöphel had mastery not only over both sutra and tantra texts, but would also take a great interest even in small things such as insects.

He did not live for more than twelve years in India. He was a member of the Mahabodhi Society of India. He returned to Tibet through Bhutan. First the Bhutanese officials and later the British officials became angry with him. Their anger was further fuelled by Kashöpa's schismatic acts. It was his bad luck. They all joined together to brand him a "communist". In Kalimpong, nothing was heard of Gendün Chöphel being served a notice by the police.

Apo Rabga's letter addressed as "To the Tibetan government and the Three Monastic Seats" contained Gendün Chöphel's name but not his signature. The list of members submitted by Apo Rabga also contained names of other innocent people in Lhasa who showed a slight interest in modern reforms.

Rupön Lobzang Namgyal of the Drapchi Regiment later turned into a staunch communist. He had sent a letter to Gendün Chöphel two days before his imprisonment. It was by chance that I got hold of this letter. If this had fallen into the hands of the Tibetan government, Chöphel could have been cut into pieces. The letter was quite long and was solely concerned with revolution. By the grace of the Three Jewels, the letter landed in my hands. I quickly burned it. While burning the letter, I felt very fearful, thinking that if anyone appeared suddenly, he would notice the smell.

If he was subjected to fair trial, it would have been good. Even if he had been a communist, it would have been sensible if his opponents had opposed him with a clear understanding of communism. Without knowing the facts, some people called him "communist". Even some abbots of monasteries demanded that such people (communist supporters) must be killed and buried under the walls around Jokhang of Lhasa. If they said so, why not others?

Gendün Chöphel had compiled a work based on Tunhuang documents about Tibetan history up to the time of King Tri Ralpachen. It was an excellent work. He had described the manner in which the Tibetan king and his ministers held meetings, and the Chinese officials' manner of sitting and speaking and their facial expressions. He had also guessed how the Tibetan king and ministers had acted at that time. He had composed songs and sang them, saying that hey might have been sung like this. He said, "In Amdo, we have a song called *sba glu*, and this song should be sung in the same way, in terms of its metric style."

It was not at Nangtseshak where he was flogged. It was in the investigation room at Evam Lhogyü where he was given a light physical punishment. Hearsay had it that his friend (the co-accused) wore a beautiful piece of jewelry, which attracted the attention of Kashöpa's wife. I do not know if that was true; I don't have any proof. Both Gendün Chöphel and he were imprisoned together. However, the co-accused was released, not more than a week later, only after having offered to part with the jewelry (and satisfied Kashöpa).

Gendün Chöphel did not stay long at the monastery. He stayed there only through the course beginning with the level of Seventy Points *(don bdun bcu)* until the level of the *Old Treatise on the Middle Way (dbu ma rnying pa)*. His arguements during a debate on the refutation of "self" in the old treatise of the Middle Way at Loseling College created a controversy. During the debate, one of his opponents was called Minyak Kyorpön, who was from Minyak. He was quite proficient in the scriptures. He later became a spiritual teacher of Kashöpa. While debating with Gendün Chöphel, he suddenly lost ground. He might have volunteered to rise first to debate against Gendün Chöphel, saying that he would challenge him. When Minyak Kyorpön failed to sustain the debate any further, a slightly crazy and shabbily dressed Mongolian Geshe from our monastic college rose up and shouted, "Hai! Ri, Ri! Ri! Ri!" He even took his worn-out shawl off to wipe Minyak Kyorpön's face and bragged loudly. This appeared to embarrassed Minyak Kyorpön at that time. When Kashöpa later turned against Gendün Chöphel, Minyak Kyorpön was suspected of having stirred up Kashöpa. But I don't think that being an exceptionally great Geshe, Minyak Kyorpön would not stoop to such an ugly act. It was entirely Kashöpa's misdemeanor, and there were other factors as well.

Generally, when it was time for debate, we would study the scriptures very seriously. But, when we reminded Gendün Chöphel of the forthcoming debate and urged him to read some scriptures, he would never listen. When there was just a month to go, he would spend only a short time skimming the texts. He just wandered around the monastery premises or spent time drawing pictures. He indeed had a black metal box, which I remember very clearly. Later it fell into the hands of *drungtsi* committee. I think his manuscripts on Tibetan history were kept by Kashöpa

After Gendün Chöphel's release from the prison, he seemed to be suffering from hypertension. Kashöpa's son used to frighten Gendün Chöphel in different wasy. I heard that he asked his servants to run hurriedly to Gendün Chöphel and tell him that the police were coming to arrest him. This would make Gendün Chöphel panic and scream. Sometimes, when Gendün Chöphel was fast asleep in the middle of the night, they would prod his head with sticks rolled in pieces of cloth. They later revealed how this frightened him so much that he would become unconsciousness.

If there were any good scholars or high lamas, Kashöpa would do everything to keep them at his place. To him Gendün Chöphel was just like a toy. He disregarded the law of karma. I personally witnessed all these things.

At the time something happened that brought a bad name to Gendün Chöphel. He was said to have kept a rubber mannequin of a woman. I thought that he might have had one, but it did not belong to him.

He initially allowed me to go near his black box, but later forbade me. A man called Lobzang Phuntsok used to smoke opium. I wondered whether the box contained accessories for smoking opium or other things that belonged to Lobzang Phuntsok. He was a member of the lamasery section of Meru Ta Lama. Most of the accusations against Gendün Chöphel such as his being a Nyingmapa were initiated by Lobzang Phuntsok. He was an opium addict and was very talkative. He was also responsible for bringing a bad name to Gendün Chöphel.

If I were asked whether Gendün Chöphel was a Gelukpa, I would say he was not. He was an impartial ecumenical practitioner. He had deep faith in the three Sakya, Geluk and Nyingma traditions, and hence could not be a communist. In retrospect, I can say that he did not belong to the Nyingma School, but he had liking for the Jonang tradition. He saw a great similarity between Jonangpa's view on the immanent state of the "Body of Perfect Resources (Sambhogakaya, longs sku)" and the non-Buddhist view of Shiva as the creator of the world. He liked this view, and he did not take much interest in Gelukpa and Nyingmapa's views. He was not biased towards any religion or philosophical position. This is because he had a perfect understanding of all philosophical viewpoints.

At the time of his arrest, there was not a single forged 100-rupee note to be seen. There had been a case a few years before that. It was just a false accusation against him. His artistic skills could have made him a good target for such accusations. At that time, there was a Mongolian sculptor who was highly skilled in carving and designing corals. Later there were rumours that he was responsible for the forgery. I think it was true. Unable to remain there, the Mongolian artist finally went to Kalimpong. Although he should have been arrested and questioned along with Gendün Chöphel, only Gendün Chöphel was produced at the trial. Some people used to say that [the Mongolian man] escaped by giving his jade necklace or something else.

On the one hand, Gendün Chöphel was alleged to be a communist spy. He was accused of holding communist views. During those days, Rabga and his associates were proposing the plan of creating a "New" Tibet. They must have sought advice from Gendün Chöphel, as he had a great interest in political issues. He told me that Tibet would progress after reform, but it would have to undergo many crises during the implementation of the progressive reform measures. It would not be wrong to say that what he said was a prediction. He said, "A huge problem will arise between the new and the old. Revolution is never an easy task." His thoughts were far-sighted. He was, therefore, not a person who would thoughtlessly call for reforms, even if there were a considerable number of people supporting them.

He met the girl who was living with him in the prison. I do not know what happened to them later. She was the only girl in his life. I do not know what he did to gain experience when he composed *Arts of Lovemaking*. She was the only girl we saw living with him as his wife. She was said to be from a good family, and I saw no shortcomings in her.

Many people used to visit him to either ask questions or have discussions mainly on the Middle Way (Madhyamika) or on the

Mind-Only (Cittamatra) philosophy. Ngawang Dhondup also used to come. A man named Gojo Abu Lachung, who was probably a member of the Nyingma tradition, also used to visit him. He had written a commentary on the *Praise to Twenty-one Taras (sgrol ma nyer gcig ma'i bstod pa)*. When Trijang Rinpoche saw the commentary, he was surprised and complimented the author, saying that he had a good grasp on the Dzokchen teaching.

Two years after Gendün Chöphel left India, I came here. He died six months after I arrived in India. I was his most frequent visitor before he was imprisoned. My elder brother was the second most frequent visitor, but he did not study any particular scriptures with him. Dawa Zangpo was the only one who came for scriptural lessons. Samdup Phodrang's family cared for him well. The murals of their new house were done by him. He had painted a very fine image of King Songtsen Gampo. His one important patron was Horkhang family. For a time he even lived at one of Horkhang's residences.

Gendün Chöphel's health broke down afterwards. He might be suffering from excess fluid in his body due to his weak heart. The Chinese school (in Lhasa) asked him to work in their school. He refused their request, saying that he was not well and also that he was not qualified to teach as his knowledge was not good. He added that though the Chinese government was very kind to offer him a job, his body was too weak to do the work. Actually he could do the work as he was not too ill, but he did not accept the request. If someone else was in his place, he would have accepted the proposal, as he had suffered tremendously in prison.

As soon as Gendün Chöphel returned from India, he was in great demand among the people. Everybody worried that they would not get a chance to meet him. Sampho invited him to his house. Horkhang also did. I too invited him. Some thoughtless people came to see him just to discuss insignificant issues, because they saw others doing it. Some showed up and spoke about funny things, which I cannot recall here.

When he was imprisoned, only Horkhang and I showed up, even though others knew about it. Regent Taktra Rinpoche and Trijang Rinpoche did a lot to help him. Gendün Chöphel later told us how many presents he received from them when he was in prison. They were really great. After he was released, many people started visiting him, but he would often go to see Kyabje Rinpoche.

Gendün Chöphel seemed to have a good understanding of the Tantras. Sometimes, he and Kyabje Rinpoche used to discuss various topics such as the *champaka* flower mentioned in the Chakrasamvara for hours at a stretch. I heard this from Gendün Chöphel, as well as from Kyabje Rinpoche. The former throne-holder of Ganden Minyak Tongpön Rinpoche helped him a lot. When the two were discussing Tantric topics, it was amazing. Speaking about the lama, he would burst out laughing. He said, "He is such a great lama! He has lived in Lhasa for so many years, but he does not even know the rate of rise in the price of daily commodities over the years, not to mention other things." He continued, "He would ask me to come and chat with him. He would take three *zho* coins (a unit of Tibetan money) from under his mattress and give them to his servant to buy a few small *tenshim (tan zhim)* snacks from the market. It is impossible to get *tenshim* for just three *zho*s in the whole of Lhasa. His attendant would just glance at me, smile and leave. In a few minutes, he would bring some tenshim and place them in front of us."

"Rinpoche always drinks only one cup of tea in a bowl from his Tantric Monastery. He does not drink more than one cup. In a friendly manner, he would place the tea-kettle on a brazier close to me. Trijang Rinpoche would pick one piece of *tenshim*, bite it and give the other half to me, saying it was tasty."

I guess that Gendün Chöphel paid at least two visits to Minyak Tri Rinpoche every month. He used to spend the whole day there. This Tri Rinpoche is the ex-throne-holder of Ganden who later stayed at Tsechokling after his retirement.

As a side issue, I would like to tell a short story about Minyak Tri Rinpoche. At that time there were many Chinese workers in Lhasa. Rinpoche was said to have shed tears when he saw them. He sadly said, "Pity them; they have no right to eat what they are sowing. Look at our peasant girls. They plough the fields and appear fortunate, but they have no ownership over their harvest."

He became sick soon afterwards. Before his death, he said "Now it is the time for the throne-holder of Ganden to die. If I don't behave carefully, I may bring disrepute to the former and future throne-holders of Ganden." In his final moments, he asked for the three sets of religious robes. People saw a statue of Vajrabhairava with him. Draped in his three robes, he sat in a cross-legged meditative posture. Then sounding "Phat!" he passed away. On the windowpane opposite and at the level of statue's heart, people saw a small hole as big as a needle's thickness!

Gendün Chöphel received care from the best lamas. People who had a great quest for knowledge were dying to have him at their place. There was much confusion in his life. Sometimes he was praised very highly, while at other times, he was criticised. The people did these included geshes and aristocrats everywhere. Many geshes disliked him intensely. They considered him a follower of the Nyingmapa tradition. The geshes hated him mainly because they believed he was communist. Later I met some of them, and they told me that they were very close with Gendün Chöphel, but they did not look trustworthy.

From a very young age, Gendün Chöphel had many amazing perceptions. Before he was taken to prison, he had very frightening hallucinations.

He would narrate *Avadana-kalpa-lata* in a very tuneful Amdo tone and say "We Amdo people would sing it like that. It sounded very pleasant." There was a very learned abbot from Dhitsa, who took care of him. He was very mischievous in his childhood. He then went to Tashikhyil, where he also behaved roughly. He became a *dob-dob* (rough monk)[7] and indulged in fighting. As he was quite creative, he once made an innovative toy steam-driven airplane. During debate seasons, he would secretly devise new logical arguments, which would leave his opponents dumbfounded. He became a *dob-dob* monk at that time, and was very aggressive. He remained as *dob-dob* for a long while at Drepung Monastery.

When his father died, Gendün Chöphel was perhaps seven or eight years old. He related events about how Serkong Tsenzhab Rinpoche addressed the *dakinis* who came to escort Serkong Dorji

Chang Rinpoche on his death. The present Tsenshab Rinpoche told me that Gendün Chöphel used to say, "Today my father will make a *tshok* offering, and there will be much to see." He must have been very young at that time. Rinpoche continued that when asked what would happen during the offerings, he would say, "Many boys and girls dressed in beautiful *chupa* will sing and dance." Later when his father died, Gendün Chöphel cried that young boys and girls were taking his father with them. Tsenzhab Rinpoche had such interesting experiences to share. He is the reincarnation of Serkong Dorji Chang's ritual attendant and the son of his younger wife. Although Rinpoche did not tell me, he clearly remembers the splendid butter-sculptures he had created for Serkong Dorji Chang's Kalachakra initiation at Tsethang in Lhoka. He was very skilled in creating ritual butter-sculptures. Once during their conversations, Gendün Chöphel had told Rinpoche that when his father died, he had a perception of his father being taken away by many boys and girls, and that he felt very sad at that time.

Gendün Chöphel always wanted to travel to other countries. He told me that when he collected the Dunhuang documents, he had to indulge in acts that were almost comparable to stealing to get them. He had a great desire to visit France. I don't know what other places he wanted to visit.

Of languages, he knew Sanskrit, English and Pali. He spoke Sanskrit fluently. Reflecting on the early translators, he would sometimes shed tears and exclaim, "Our early translators were indeed great!" He had a great respect for the early translators. It seemed he was one of these translators in a previous life. He later translated *Baghavad Gita* and the translation was superb. If any ordinary Tibetan read it, he or she would agree with the content of the text, because it accepts rebirth or reincarnation. The most negative philosophical views were presented in the chapter titled "Concentration". The chapter contained very uncompromising views on the Vaishnava philosophical school. Shankaracharya had once used these very reasons to put Buddhists in a difficult position.

Gendün Chöphel was critical about one aspect of the Buddhist painting style. As depicted in Tibetan painting, we have read that when

Aryadeva contested against a non-Buddhist scholar, he employed a kitten and an unabashed monk to scare away a parrot and a beautiful woman that the latter had created. Gendün Chöphel was quite critical of this. He exclaimed with regret, "It is terrible! Has our Buddhist logic become so weak that we had to resort to a cat and an unabashed monk (to defend our stand). These are totally baseless and unfounded stories. If one does not know it, one should read the biographies of the Six Ornaments *(rgyan drug)*[8] and Two Excellent Ones *(mchog gnyis)*[9] composed by Taranatha. Those stories are not found in it. Those stories mar the image of Buddhism. Buddhists defeated their opponents by relying on reasoning and scriptural citations. Buddhist philosophy is not so weak as to seek help from a kitten, a brazen monk or oil."

Gendün Chöphel was, for most of the time [in India], looked after by Roerich. The reason was that he needed his help to translate the *Blue Annals*. He traveled to South India and Orissa. He also visited Kamarupa, one of the twenty-four sacred places, where he witnessed the site where [Chakrasamvara] bestowed the Fourth Initiation *(dbang bzhi pa)* and congregation with his consort. He also visited the sacred sites of Garzha (Lahual in India)[10] many times.

Gendün Chöphel met Rahul during the latter's visit to Lhasa. Rahul went to Tibet to collect Indian manuscripts. Gendün Chöphel accompanied Rahul to Sakya to help him find manuscripts. He reminisced about how they demonstrated magical tricks in front of the Sakya Dakchen Rinpoche and amazed him. They first demonstrated some magic to him and then borrowed some ancient Indian manuscripts in return. He told me that the Rinpoche was fond of magic. He revealed to us the secrets of some of their magic tricks. In one of their tricks, they filled a cylindrical bamboo stick with egg yolk and then sealed the ends with frozen butter. Since Gendün Chöphel had dexterous hands, he must have done these tricky things. They first showed the bamboo stick to the Rinpoche. They then heated a pan on which they moved the stick with its mouth down several times. After a while, the butter melted, releasing the egg through its opening, thereby making an omelet on the pan. As they offered the omelet to Rinpoche, one of his attendants stopped them. He himself tested it and exclaimed, "It is real egg!" They also played tricks using boxes. In one such trick, they hid money in one corner of a box, leaving the other corners empty. After tricking them for a while, they produced the money and offered it to the Rinpoche. But the Rinpoche refused, saying, "This is not real money, it will disappear." They confounded the Rinpoche in such ways. When the Rinpoche asked for more tricks, they said they had to observe serious magical rites for new tricks. They followed no rites, so it was only an excuse for them to have more time to copy the manuscripts borrowed from the Rinpoche.

Notes

1. Tibetan: nub bod legs bcos kyi skyid sdug, whose English name was the Tibetan Revolutionary Party, or Tibet Improvement Party.
2. Acronym for drungyig chenmo and tsipon; drungyig chenmo refers to the four monk officials of the Tsé Yigtsang and tsipon refers to the four lay officials of the Finance Department of the traditional Tibetan government.
3. Tibetan: 'byor-lcag dang thon-lcag
4. In 1947, when the Reting Rinpoche was arrested on charges of plotting to remove the Regent Taktra, the monks of Sera and Reting monasteries resorted to violence to release him.
5. Dawa Zangpo was a Japanese spy, who visited Tibet in the disguise of a Mongolian monk. His real name was Hisao Kimura. See his autobiography *Japanaese Agent in Tibet*, London: Serindia Publications.
6. Chinese Muslims are called Huihui.
7. Dob-dob is a monk who is generally robust and engages in fighting and other non-academic works; these monks are used as labours and sometimes as police force to maintain law and order at monasteries or during ceremonies. Bigger monasteries even have dob-dob associations.
8. Nagarjuna, Aryadeva, Asanga, Vasubhandu, Dignaga, and Dharmakirti.
9. Nagarjuna and Asanga.
10. Garzha is a Tibetan name for Lahaul, a district in Himachal Pradesh, India.

Why was Gendün Chöphel imprisoned?

Tashi Palrab*

The Nangtseshak Office *(snang rtse shag gi las khungs)* functioned as the city court as well as the security office of Lhasa town. It handled various civil and criminal cases which arose within the town. If there were serious or important cases, the Kashak (Cabinet of Ministers) would summon the two magistrates *(mi dpon)* and give them instructions on how to deal with the matter. When Gendün Chöphel was arrested, Shakjang Zurpa *(shag byang zur pa)* and I were the two magistrates. The Kashak summoned us and instructed us, "There is a man named Amdo Gendün Chöphel in Lhasa. Our government has strong suspicions about this person, so you must trace him and arrest him." We did not know Gendün Chöphel's whereabouts, so we replied that we would search for him. The Kashak further ordered us to find and arrest him that very day and seal his house. They said, "We have many reasons to arrest Gendün Chöphel, but we don't think it is necessary to tell you everything at the moment—we will let you know later. Gendün Chöphel is a great scholar, so he might ask the reasons for his arrest. In that case, you don't have to say much—just tell him that many counterfeit Tibetan 100-rupee currency notes are being found in Tibet. These fake notes have most probably come from India. It is he who has circulated them in Lhasa.

---

* Belonging to an aristocratic family in Lhasa, he became head of the Nangtseshak, the highest judiciary of Tibet. Nangtseshak was the chief security office of the Tibetan Government and was responsible for all matters relating to prisons and criminals. When Gendün Chöphel was arrested, Kungo Tashi Palrab was the official in charge of his case. After Gendün Chöphel was freed, Tashi Palrab learned some poetry texts like "gZhon-nu-zla-med-kyi-gtam" from him. Due to this, he had intimate knowledge of Gendün Chöphel's prison days.

So he is being arrested on this charge. This is not the real reason; there are other reasons."

As the heads of the Security Office of Lhasa we were ex officio the heads of the Lhasa Police Force. We went to the Lhasa police station located at Tromsikhang *(khrom gzigs khang)*. There were some policemen there. We asked them if they knew Gendün Chöphel. Some of them knew him and told us that he was staying at Wangden Pelbar House, a building owned by the Kündeling family, near the Police Station. We sent some of them to see if he was there. They came back and reported to us that his room was locked and he had gone to Horkhang's residence.

Horkhang's son was a senior officer in the Bodyguard Regiment of the Tibetan army. He had always had an interest in learning poetry, and Gendün Chöphel used to go to his house to teach him. I sent the policemen to Horkhang's residence to check if he was there. They returned and said that they had been told he had come there in the morning and left with Mr. Horkhang for the Bodyguard Regiment at Norbulingka, and that he would return to his residence that evening.

We waited for him. We instructed the gatekeepers of the army camp to inform us when he left. At around three in the afternoon, we received a message that he had arrived at his house. We immediately sent two officers and a clerk to bring him to Nangtseshak, with a message that the two magistrates wanted to see him. He appeared before us within a short time. We told him that we had received an order from the Kashak to keep him in custody at the Nangtseshak for the time being. We explained to him that he was under suspicion of smuggling counterfeit 100-rupee Tibetan currency notes into Lhasa and that he would have to remain there for a few days for investigation. Gendün Chöphel responded,

> I have done nothing to arouse suspicion. Except for a small house, I have nothing. But it's the government's order. You can keep me anywhere you like; I have to obey your orders. However, my little house will surely be searched. There is nothing special in it; there are many manuscripts, books and scraps of papers with notes, scattered all around, as I am writing a Tibetan history for the benefit of the people

of Tibet. I have written notes even on cigarette wrappers. So please take care to leave those things the way they are, after searching the room. While enduring great hardship, I visited various places in India and collected ancient manuscripts on Tibet. I have copied all those that are authentic and made notes from all those that are important, using even empty cigarette cases. So I possess a large number of notes. You can examine them, but leave them where they are. I have always thought of doing something for Tibet; I have not been doing anything wrong. Everything will become clear after the investigation. Kindly tell this to your superiors. So today, I will do whatever you say.

We took him to Nangtseshak prison, which had different types of cells. On the top floor, adjacent to the conference room, there was a small room used as a rest room for high officials. We kept him in that room. We did not handle him harshly, claiming that we had orders from the Kashak.

After that, we reported the entire matter to the Kashak: "As per the Kashak's instruction, we made inquiries about the whereabouts of Gendün Chöphel. We learned that he is living at Wangden Pelbar's house. We did not find him there and we were told that he had gone to Horkhang's house to give tuition to Horkhang's son, who is an army officer. When we checked if he was there, he had just left for the Bodyguard Regiment at Norbulingka. After he returned to his residence, we called him to our office. We explained to him in detail why he was arrested and taken into custody. He told us that he had committed no offences and explained what he was doing nowadays. He requested that if his room was searched, we should leave his papers scribbled with notes scattered everywhere in his room as they were after the examination. He is in our custody at the moment."

The Kashak said, "Well done. However, don't allow him to have access to visitors or letters. You should assign your two prison guards, turn by turn, to guard him. It is totally wrong if you allow him to do whatever he likes, considering that he is in custody." Accordingly, we deployed two guards in shifts and instructed them not to allow anyone to visit Gendün Chöphel.

After about two weeks, the Kashak appointed an investigating committee to question him about the charges against him. The committee consisted of Dzasak Gyaltakpa *(dza sag rgyal stag pa)*, the Junior Zurkhang *(zur khang gi sku gzhon mda' dpon)* who was an army leader in the rank of dapon, and a manager from the government's treasury in Lhasa *(lhasa gnyer tshang pa)*. The venue where they conducted the investigation was the government office known as the Treasury Office, located close to the Tsuglakhang temple. The office was generally called "Lhogyü" (Southern Quarter) and it was the trial venue for VIP detainees. Gendün Chöphel was summoned and interrogated daily in that room. When we asked him what he had explained to the investigating committee, he replied, "I have nothing new to explain other than what I had told you before, but they are not satisfied. Just think." With great frustration, he continued, "Whatever they say, even if they flay the skin off me, I have nothing more to say."

Then after a gap of two days, we received an order to send him to the investigating committee. We sent him escorted by some guards. That trial session involved a very harsh cross-examination and he may have been given several floggings. When he returned to us, he looked extremely depressed. He told us that he was tortured during the trial. There was nothing that we could do. Strangely, through some karmic power my wife felt an immense sense of empathy towards him when she heard his name for the first time. So when I went home and told her that he had been tortured during the trial, she immediately prepared special food and sent it to him.

Early the next morning I squeezed my head into the peephole of his cell and asked if he was given physical punishment during the last session. He replied that he was. He said that even if they killed or beheaded him, he had nothing new to add to what he had already told us earlier. He added that he was very upset. I tried to console him, saying, "It does not matter. You should not worry. Sometimes such things happen. Since you have travelled to many foreign countries, it could arouse suspicion. Nothing bad will happen to you. Under our Tibetan law, everything will be investigated thoroughly and everything will ultimately become clear. If you have committed no offence to feel guilty about, no one can blacken your name. You shouldn't worry." I tried to cheer him up with these words. He thanked me profusely for my encouragement. After that, the investigating committee did not summon him again.

Later, when it was close to the Tibetan New Year, we transferred all the prisoners at Nangtseshak to Zhöl prison, as it was mandatory by law not to keep any prisoners there during the Tibetan New Year festival. Gendün Chöphel was also transferred. They were brought back to Nangtseshak after the Great Mönlam Festival was over. He also returned to Nangtseshak.

One day, while at Nangtseshak prison, Gendün Chöphel became slightly ill. He told us that he was not well. Giving us a piece of paper which had the names of some medicines written in English, he asked us to bring them to him. We did not know English. Since it was a great risk for us to give him such medicines without the consent of the Kashak, we showed the slip to the Kashak and told them that Gendün Chöphel was not well and that he had asked us to bring him the medicines written on the slip. Far from giving us permission, they reprimanded us harshly, saying, "How did he get the pen and paper to write? We had instructed the two of you not to allow him to have access to either people or things. You have been very lenient with him. He has kept with him all the instruments with which he can do anything that he likes. This is a very serious matter." (Kashöpa, Zurkhang and Rampa were the cabinet ministers at that time.)

My colleague and I always performed our duties, such as guarding the prisoners, in accordance with the Kashak's orders. We did not let anybody visit him in the prison secretly, openly or indirectly. We were not allowed to do so. However, since we had heard that some Indian medicines cause sudden death, we dared not give him the medicines. So unable to take the risk, we showed the slip given us by him to the Kashak; we did not do anything wrong. It was not that we did not guard him. Since we did not know English, we asked the Kashak. That we had been too lenient with him was not true.

Kashöpa reprimanded us severely, saying, "You two officers are giving Gendün Chöphel too much freedom—it is not right." Just before we left, Surkhang said, "The two magistrates have come here only to consult us, as they were not able to decide themselves. They are right. There is nothing wrong in it. The slip is not a letter—it just contains the names of medicines. They are asking us whether they should give the medicines to him or not. There is no reason we should reprimand them. It's alright." He concluded the matter.

About three months later, we were called to the Kashak. The ministers told us that though Gendün Chöphel had been kept at Nangtseshak prison, so far they had not gained any satisfactory information from him, despite the fact that the investigating committee had questioned him using both gentle and harsh methods. Therefore, he should be handed over to Zhöl prison for the time being. Accordingly, we sent Gendün Chöphel, escorted by our two guards, to Zhöl prison. There, he did not face any torture or cross-examination during his prison term.

Then, on the occasion of the enthronement ceremony of His Holiness the 14th Dalai Lama (in 1950), a general amnesty was granted to all prisoners in Tibet. Gendün Chöphel was also released on that day. He had spent three years in prison.

As soon as he was released, he came to my house and thanked me, saying, "You were quite lenient and kind to me during my stay at Nangtseshak prison. I did not suffer injustice and unfair trials, nor did I hear or see a prisoner being harassed or tortured in the prison. I like you very much. I cannot repay your kindness in any way, but as I have a little knowledge, how about teaching you some texts?" I responded, "That would be very good. Although we did not know each other before, I knew from seeing you that you were not the kind of person who does bad things. My colleague and I both shared the same view. Therefore, although the Kashak had ordered us to be very strict with you, we were somewhat lenient. Now you have nothing to regret or fear."

He then asked me about his manuscripts and documents. I forgot to mention one thing earlier - when Gendün Chöphel was at Nangtseshak, the Kashak summoned the two of us and instructed us to bring all the documents and papers from Gendün Chöphel's room to the Kashak. I answered, "It is not going to be easy to bring all of them together in front of you, because he told us that he collected all those old manuscripts while travelling through many places in India, enduring great hardships, and he requested us to leave them as they were. If a single loose page is lost, he will not be able to complete his book. So, they might be very important. Shouldn't we examine them and leave them there?" They said, "Okay then, go and examine the documents."

We went to his room and examined all the documents. There was not a single suspicious document. There was a document containing the names of all the Tibetan government's offices, including the Kashak. He had written the names of the officers and workers in each office. It carried the names of ministers of the Kashak, secretaries of the Tsé Yigtsang Office, staff of the Lhasa Treasury and so forth. The rest of the writings contained matters relating to the country's border issues, the White Stupa of China and so on. In terms of his belongings, he had two robes and a few shirts. There were four hundred Indian rupees under his mattress. The easiest document to take was the one containing the list of the Tibetan government's offices and officials. So we took it and gave it to the Kashak. They asked us if we had seen any documents carrying the Russian Bolshevik logo. We replied that we had not found any such papers.

The Kashak then instructed us to bring the remaining documents as well. I expressed my concern over the risk of losing those documents, which might contain important matters helpful to our government in the future. The Kashak insisted that we bring them, saying that nothing would happen to them. So I put all the papers into a big sack and took it to the Kashak. Later, (after his release) when Gendün Chöphel came to my house and asked me about his manuscripts, I explained to him that we collected all of them and gave them to the Kashak. I added, "We took great care not to lose even a single scrap of paper in the process. I put everything in a big sack. Although those papers are not in the same position that you had kept them in your house before, we did not lose even one of them. You should be able to complete your work now. I will request the Kashak to give them back; I am sure that they will return them, as those documents are for the purpose of academic writing. You should continue your work." He sadly said, "Now everything is over. Nothing can be done. Even if all the documents are there and the Kashak gives them to you, I have already lost my mind and I can never complete the work. Let them give the notes to anyone they like—I don't need them anymore. I just asked you about this matter as a friend. Now nothing can be done. It is a great disaster. I collected those notes while enduring great difficulties."

Not long after that he started drinking regularly. As mine was a middle class family, neither too rich nor too poor, we always had liquor at our house to be served to guests. Gendün Chöphel used to address my wife as "Ama Katrinchen (Kind Mother)." Saying that he wanted to meet us often, he used to come to our house everyday and ask for liquor. When he was completely drunk, he would lie on a bed. We used to chat for hours. Once during one of our chats, he said, "It was not the Kashak's fault, I know the main culprit responsible for my imprisonment. When I asked him who he was, he answered that he would tell me later. A few days later, when he came to my house, I said, "Last time you promised to tell me the name of the person who caused your arrest. Please tell me who he was; it will be amusing to know. The person could not harm you much." He said:

> Okay, the one who tried to "put a black hat on a white person"[1] was none other than the British diplomat Richardson[2], who resides at Dekyilingka." He instigated the Kashak to act. The reason was that when I went to British India (? dbyin ji'i lung pa) I translated a book in English. The translation was very good. As my English is very good, the British government asked me to stay and work for them, saying they would give me a good salary. I refused. From that day on, they started to dislike me. Richardson is a British man and he asked me some questions earlier. I could judge from his facial expression that he hated me on sight. So he poisoned the minds of Kashöpa and Surkhang against me, and they in turn reported it to the Kashak. The Kashak arrested and imprisoned me on trumped up charges. It was all due to Richardson.

> When I was in Kalimpong I met Rabga, son of Pomdatsang family. He studies traditional Tibetan subjects on his own, and also asks knowledgeable people to teach him. He is a very peculiar man. I stayed at his house for many days. He told me that it would be of no use if I returned to Tibet. He asked me to stay there and he would

> give me a monthly stipend. You must have found 400 or 500 Indian rupees in my room.

I replied, "Yes, we found them, and we spent them for you. We two magistrates did not use them for our own purposes, nor did the government take them. Sometimes, I brought food to you from my house, and we gave some money to the two guards to buy you food." He continued:

> The money was sent to me by Rabga on a monthly basis. Our government does not like Pomda Rabga. The Kashak knew where the money came from, and therefore they attacked me. I have never done anything bad at any time in my life.

After that, his emotional crisis worsened day by day. After His Holiness the 14th Dalai Lama assumed both spiritual and temporal leadership of Tibet, Gendün Chöphel was allocated a room in the building of the Department of Agriculture, located close to the Kashak. He was also granted a monthly salary. During his stay there, we repeatedly implored him to complete his unfinished book on Tibetan history, but he turned a deaf ear. He gathered some students and taught them at his house. He did nothing special apart from this. The ones who were closest to him at that time were the Samdrup Phodrang family. The late Kalön Samdrup Phodrang was a very learned man, and he looked after Gendün Chöphel very kindly. Sampho used to visit him very often and study scriptures with him. Although many people from all walks of life including government officials used to visit him occasionally, Samdrup Phodrang and my family were the closest to him. After he got a room and started receiving a monthly stipend, he once said to me, "Through the kindness of His Holiness the Dalai Lama, I am very happy now, but my mind is not sound."

Gendün Chöphel's arrest took place, probably in the seventh or eighth Tibetan month, at the end of summer. He did not remain at Nangtseshak prison for long; he was soon moved to Zhöl prison. According to the law, in winter time all the prisoners at Nangtseshak prison had to be relocated to Zhöl prison. He was arrested alone and there were no co-accused with him. When we arrested him, we did not put handcuffs or restraints on him. At first we two magistrates waited for him at the police station at Tromsigkhang for a few hours. After that we went the Army Headquarters, from where we summoned him from Wangden Pelbar's house. When he came to us, he was wearing a burgundy woollen chupa. We explained to him the reasons why we had summoned him. Then we took him to Nangtseshak prison. There we had prison cells underground with very bad conditions for ordinary prisoners. We did not put him there; we kept him in a room on the upper floor. We never handled him harshly. During the trial, he was given 25-30 floggings. We accompanied him everywhere and treated him like a normal man—we did not handcuff him or tie his hands with ropes.

During the trial, he was accused of acting as a Russian spy. I don't know what questions were asked by the investigating committee during the investigation. During one of the trial sessions, he was tortured and he looked very upset. The next day, I went to my office early and consoled him. I asked him what charges the investigating committee had made against him, and he seemed a bit confused and frustrated, as he recalled, "First, they told me that I have brought many counterfeit 100-rupee notes into Tibet. Secondly, they told me that I am a Russian spy. They asked me how I formed an alliance with the Russians. I told them what I told you and your colleague before—I have nothing else to say."

The investigating committee questioned him mildly for about four days. As he said nothing special, they reported to the Kashak that they had not got any significant information from him. Kashöpa ordered them to use harsh methods, saying there was no other option. It was only under the instruction of the Kashak that the investigating committee resorted to a harsh trial—it was not their own decision, because Zurkhang Dapön, one of the members of the investigating committee, was very friendly with Gendün Chöphel.

Gendün Chöphel shared many of his personal stories with me during our conversations. One time he told me:

> Before I was arrested, Kashöpa regarded me like his root lama *(rtsa ba'i bla ma)* and treated me very kindly. But later, influenced by others, he imprisoned me for no reason. He drove me mad. Both

Zurkhang and Kashöpa were responsible for this. One day, after my release, Kashöpa invited me to his house. First I declined. He again sent his servant to me, with a request that I should visit his house that very day. So I went. When I arrived at his house, he came down the stairs to receive me. He said, "You faced great troubles in the recent past, and I was compelled to take such actions against you because the case concerned the country's security. We tried to handle you softly as we could." He pretended to have done this for my own good. I replied, "That does not matter—it might be my fate. I am totally innocent and have never sought help from outside people to do anything against my country. Whether you handled me gently or not, you have already made me mentally ill—you have transformed a normal person into an abnormal one." He insisted that I go into his house and stay for a while. I went in and he served me tea and liquor. I drank the liquor and ate some food. He told me that I should visit him whenever and for whatever I needed. I replied, "I will not stay in your house as I have my own house granted by His Holiness. I came to your house today because you sent your servant twice to fetch me. If you call me again, I will have nothing to say to you and I would prefer not to come here. Today I stayed here for a while at your insistence. I have nothing to request from you in future." I never went to his place again."

He then told me, "One day Surkhang invited me to his house and received me very warmly saying, "Venerable teacher, please come in." He recollected:

> They had arranged a very grand feast and there were many types of food and drink. After a while, he gave me a piece of paper and asked me to draw a beautiful picture on it. When asked what I should draw, he said I could draw whatever I wished, whether an image of the Buddha or anything else. I thought of drawing a good image of the Buddha. I put the paper on the table and took a pen. Then, while I was talking, I first drew a circle. Looking at the shape of the circle, I thought it would make a picture of an animal. As I drew further, it became a beautiful donkey. I told him that a strange picture had come out and showed it to him. He looked at it and remarked that it was beautiful. He did not ascribe any meaning to the picture. He suggested that it would look nice if there was a saddle on the animal. I said it was easy to draw a saddle and I drew one. I also drew a high-pointed hood-like hair-lock on the donkey's

head. Slowly the donkey began to look more spruced up. Then he suggested that a man be drawn near the donkey instead of leaving it alone. I said that it was very easy to draw a man. I drew a man on the donkey's rear, instead of placing him in the normal position. His right hand was near the donkey's bottom. From that I suddenly got a bad idea. I drew a chopping knife in his hand. When I showed him the completed picture, he burst out laughing, but he also seemed to be slightly uncomfortable. I had a funny thought about the picture. To me it seemed to symbolize the saying, "The shameless master kills and eats his donkey," implying that they (those who imprisoned him) initially treated me as a lama, but later arrested and imprisoned me."

Once he told me that Zurkhang's younger brother, who was a regimental leader *(mda' dpon)* of the Drapchi Regiment, was very fond of him. He recalled,

He always calls me to his house. He does not ask anything about political issues. He asks me about religious topics. Although I am not able to teach as I used to do before, still I try to teach him as much as I can. He is a good man. Surkhang's youngest brother is a monk official with the title "Tsedrön Khenchung". Though he always says he wants to learn scriptures, he is not learning anything from me. But still he gives me money and looks after me. These two younger brothers are very kind to me. So I always go to Zurkhang's residence. Every time I go there, they give me money, with which I buy groceries and other things.

Gendün Chöphel had a wife, a woman from Kham, whom he met during his stay at Zhöl prison. She was not a sophisticated lady. She only knew about cooking. She did not talk much. He told me that she was good at cooking and he gave her money to buy food ingredients. Sometimes I took foodstuffs to him. Although initially my family used to give him food and other daily necessities, later he refused to take them from us, saying he received enough from Zurkhang and others.

He persuaded me several times to study some Buddhist texts with him. Although he was a really learned man, I procrastinated since I did not have any enthusiasm for studying the scriptures. I told him I was too lazy for such rigorous study. He advised me that I could just try studying the texts and I could stop it whenever I found it boring. As I was young, I had no interest in such things. I told him that all I wanted to learn was English. He suggested that I first study scriptures for at least a year, and only then would he teach me English. He advised me that I could learn English slowly. He said, "I also learned English this way. I had never been to school to learn English. First, do what I tell you. Learn do what I teach you. You can stop the lesson if ever you feel like going out or playing games. I will never force you to study. If you really want to learn English, you can learn it. For example, if you want to go to Chushül, you have to first walk through Kyangtang Nakha, then to Denbak. Then gradually passing through Trizam bridge, you will finally reach Chushül. There is no expressway to reach Chushül straightaway. So just do as I say—first learn the scriptural texts and I can guarantee that you will pick up English really well after that."

However, I never studied Buddhist texts with Gendün Chöphel. In those days, it was difficult to find the text called *gzhon nu zla med kyi rtogs brjod* (Tale of the Prodigy Boy). I had one part of the text in the form of a roll, and the other part was with Ragashak. I kept the text on my altar. One day he asked me what it was. I told him it was a text called *gzhon nu zla med kyi rtogs brjod*. He said it was a very interesting story. I told him that I couldn't understand any of it despite having read it several times. He asked me not to worry at all. Then lying back on a pillow on the bed opposite me, he smoked a cigarette and drank some liquor, and asked me to read the text. I read the text paragraph by paragraph. The text was written in a poetic style, and he explained each line in detail. We repeated the entire process almost three times. Later I read it myself three times, and I was able to understand the meaning a little bit. I asked him whenever I found a difficult point in it. I noted down all the difficult terms that I did not understand and asked him. I did this three times. This was the only textual study that I ever did with Gendün Chöphel. During the lesson, when I read the text aloud, he would sometimes recite along with me from memory as if he was reading the text.

He used to drink heavily. He always had a bottle of liquor in his robes whenever he went out. One day I advised him, "Don't drink so much liquor. Your health will deteriorate. Many people die due to drinking liquor. You can drink *chang* (Tibetan wine)[3] instead. I have chang at my house all the time, so you can drink it whenever you come to my house."

I had a servant named Buné *(bu ne)*, who had not much interest in religious teachings and lamas. It was through the sheer work of karma that he was very fond of Gendün Chöphel. Buné would come to my house to work, but would suddenly disappear even if he had not finished his work. When I asked him where he had been, he would say that he had been to Gendün Chöphel's house to ask him if he needed anything. So I told Gendün Chöphel that he should quit drinking alcohol, and that even if he did not come to my house to drink, I would send him *chang* through Buné. He replied that he would never drink liquor again. I asked, "You mean you will not drink liquor from today? Are you serious?" He said, "Yes, I meant it." When he left, he gave me a four-line verse and told me to read it. The verse read:

> At the feet of the great official,
> I, Gendün Chöphel, the most inferior man,
> Swear by Songtsen Gampo that
> I will never ever drink liquor again.

After that, he only drank *chang*, not liquor, until his last breath. When we met next time he told me that he had drunk no liquor since that very afternoon when he made the promise that he wouldn't drink liquor again. He said, "From that day on after I pledged to you that I would never drink liquor, I completely stopped drinking alcohol."

Sometimes he would visit temples and would ask me to accompany him. I used to go with him whenever he asked me. He would first approach the image of Avalokitesvara. Climbing the stone steps, he would then go to Tsongkhapa's temple and then to the Jowo chapel. After that he would go to Songtsen Gampo's temple, and then say, "Our visit of worship is complete. Now let's go back." I would suggest that we offer beverage offering *(gser skyems)*[4] to the protector-deities Rudrani and Palden Lhamo in the upper chapels. He would say, "It is not necessary," and would immediately leave through the southern gate. His house was right near there and he would ask me go to his house. We would stay there for awhile and smoke cigarettes. When I left, I would ask him if he would like to come to my house the next day. His routine reply would be, "May be, I'm not sure." So he would occasionally come to my house.

Gendün Chöphel had many manuscripts, scriptural texts and books in his house. Most of them were his own works. There were many pieces of papers, rolls of Tibetan handmade papers and cigarette boxes on which he had written notes. When we handed them over to the Kashak, we put all of them in a large sack. Among them, there were ancient documents that were beyond our capacity to understand. Some of them looked very old, as if they had been unearthed from some ancient site. There were also Tibetan mantras. There were many white sacks in the Kashak's building. They contained rejected petitions and were useless. The sack containing Gendün Chöphel's documents was put in the same room. Whenever I went to the Kashak after his imprisonment, I would see the sack in that room.

I told Gendün Chöphel that his manuscripts and books were of no use to the Kashak and that I would request the Kashak to return them to him. I assured him that I would definitely get them back if he wanted. I asked him several times if he needed them. He always replied, "No, I don't need them at all." Actually, all was there intact; they had not been lost or destroyed by fire.

He did not have any black box. The weirdest thing is that he had a rubber model of a woman. He asked me not to tell others about it. He said, "I am not a monk anymore. But if I keep a wife, it will really interfere with my work. So I have brought this doll from India." I did not tell anybody about this. Except that it did not breathe, the doll was a complete woman. It could be inflated to become a life-size doll whenever he wanted. He told me that he had reasons for keeping it. He explained, "I am not a monk. So sometimes I find it difficult to suppress my mind. If I keep a real woman as my wife, I will have to spend time with her talking and cooking, which will take away my precious time that otherwise could be used for writing. So I have kept this with me to avoid these problems." When we went to ransack his house (after he was arrested), the doll was blown up. His house had two rooms and a small kitchen. He had drawn a white curtain across the door where he slept. While I remained outside examining the documents, Shakjang Zurpa checked inside the room. He saw the dummy of a woman. Gendün Chöphel had painted a woman's face on the doll and put a wig on its head that made it look like a Tibetan nomadic woman. Startled by the doll, Shakjang Zurpa shouted, "My colleague, colleague! Come here, there is a strange thing here." The reason is that he had never heard of such a thing before, let alone seen it. Though I had not personally seen before such things, I had heard about them. So I said, "These are common in foreign countries, so don't be shocked." I tore it into pieces and threw away the pieces.

In his house, there was nothing special, except for a few clothes, a table, a stool, some utensils and the rubber dummy of a woman. Except for the small area where he slept, the whole room was covered with scraps of paper and books. There were books in English. There was a small notebook containing a translation from Sanskrit. In the "Conclusion" section of the book, there was a line that read: "As we know, there were many panditas (scholars) in India in the past, but there are none there nowadays. There is only one pandita in Lhasa and he is probably Gendün Chöphel." The opening part of the text contained indecipherable scripts similar to those used for writing mantras. At the end of the book, there was a three-page translation done by Gendün Chöphel. After reading the translation, the cabinet ministers Kashöpa and Zurkhang remarked, "It is amazing to see all these texts translated into only three pages! This shows that he is really a great writer. He is a true pandita." They kept the book on their table, but all the remaining documents were kept in the sack.

As for Gendün Chöphel's signature, it was very peculiar. To a Tibetan who did not know English, it had his full name in Tibetan, while for others who knew English but not Tibetan, it carried his name in English. It was really beautiful. He was also very skilled in drawing and painting. He had drawn very beautiful murals of a lion and a tiger at the entrance of the small guesthouse of Samdrup Phodrang. If somebody went there for the first time, the pictures would look like real animals. He was a really gifted artist. Later he pretended to call himself a mad man. However, he was as mentally vigorous as before, although he did not do any work.

Before he was allotted a house by the government after his release from prison, he stayed at the Kedung House *(skad dung)*, which was located behind the Samding House. At that time, he and Minyak Kyorpön *(mi nyag skyor dpon)*, a young abbot of a Tantric college, who was said to be highly knowledgeable in scriptures, seem to have engaged in an intense debate on scriptural topics through their correspondence. Later, the abbot failed to give prompt replies and he appeared to have lost ground. Gendün Chöphel recalled:

> One day he came to my house with about eight learned monks from the Tantric College. He might have come because he had no answers to (the points I raised in letters). When I asked his purpose of the visit, he replied that he had a question to ask me. He explained that it was more convenient to talk to me personally instead of writing. 'That's fine,' I said. He looked garish to me. He was tall and fat. He wore fine robes. He reacted strangely if not addressed in a respectful manner. I once invited him to my house to conduct an ablution ritual. His attendants asked me to burn incense to purify and cleanse the room before he took his seat. He was very pompous and acted in an exaggerated manner. I asked him what he wanted to ask me. He said that I was responsible for starting the debate through correspondence, although it was actually he who started it. I asked him why he had brought the monks along with him, and he replied that they would ask me questions. I told them to ask me any questions they wished. I let them speak one by one, starting with the abbot, and remained silent until all of them had finished their questions. At the end I got up, taking a rosary in my hands, in a style typical of a debater in monastic debate sessions held in a monastic courtyard, and answered each of their questions one by one. I shut them up and sent them away. After that, they neither sent me any letters, nor did they come to my house again.

He had never talked this way before. He once told me, "At first glance the writings of Tibetan government officials give the impression that they are highly educated. But on closer observation I found that they lack even basic writing skills. It is rare to find an official who is knowledgeable."

Gendün Chöphel had deep faith in the former throne-holder of Ganden, Trizur Rinpoche (Minyak Tongpön) of Drib Tsechokling, and praised him highly, "Trizur Rinpoche is truly a great lama. He is beyond description."

He might have seen the writings of the Regent Taktra Rinpoche, because he praised the Rinpoche's writings, saying they were excellent and that such perfect writings were rare. He said, "Kashöpa and Zurkhang are just sharp-minded, and nothing more. Samdrup Phodrang is quite knowledgeable in literature and all his writings, from beginning to end, are remarkable. It is difficult to find an official who is really proficient in literature; most of them have merely learned the alphabet. Kungo Chokteng is also good in the art of writing. He is considered to be one of the best among the government staff in the field of literature. It would be good for you to study their writings. The majority of government officials know nothing."

When he was in Zhöl prison, he was kept like the rest of the prisoners and he received no special treatment as he did at Nangtseshak. But he was not handcuffed or bound by chains. Amgulak Ngawang Dhondup, Drangtöpa, a relative of Kashöpa and fourth ranking Rimzhi Sechungsé were Zhöl prison officials at that time. Later when I asked Gendün Chöphel if they treated him well, he replied, "I don't remember whether they treated me nicely or badly." He was kept there for a long time, without being given any verdict on whether he was guilty or not. He was probably held there in order to ruin his life. Thanks to the enthronement ceremony of His Holiness the 14th Dalai Lama he was released. Without this event, he probably would have remained in prison for the rest of his life. At the time of his release, someone called Ngampo Tsadi was appointed a magistrate of Lhasa and his colleague was Shödrung Gogkhar.

Gendün Chöphel had been in Lhasa for more than three years before his arrest, but there were no negative rumours about him during those years. I think the Kashak arrested him at the instigation of Richardson, who resided at Dekyilingka Park, because Gendün Chöphel later told me that it was all due to Richardson. The Kashak acted rashly by listening to Richardson. The Kashak said that Gendün

Chöphel was a Russian spy and had documents bearing the hammer & sickle logo of the USSR, although I never saw any of them at his residence. I am sure the Kashak must have wondered whether he had any such documents. We also had the same doubts at that time.

One day, sometime after his release, I asked Gendün Chöphel why he had made a list of Tibetan government offices and officials. He explained that he wrote the names of some government officials who he considered knowledgeable and good reference sources for his research works. He said that he had no other reasons besides that and that he had not sent or showed the list to anyone else. He lamented, "Even if you turn me inside out, this is all I have to say. If I don't tell you, whom should I tell?" He said Horkhang's son helped him in the preparation of the list. Chöphel had a great respect for Horkhang's son. He told me that Horkhang treated him nicely even after his release from the prison.

The money we found in his house was real Indian currency, known as Kingjor (probably King George). It was not British Sterling. The money was sent to him by Rabga. Later, when he became ill, I went to see him and gave him food and medicines. I asked him about his condition and whom he had consulted. He replied, "I am fine; I just feel lethargic and am not able go out for a walk. I have no other problems." I asked him to tell me whatever he needed. I said, "My servant always goes to your house every day." He replied, "Yes, yes, he always comes to see me." I told him, "I have instructed my servant to care for you. You can tell him to bring you whatever you want. Since I have to stay at the Army Headquarters, I am not able to visit you very often." To this he replied, "Don't worry. I will get well very soon and will surely come to your office at the Army Headquarters. I have never been there. So I always ask your servant about you. He says you are sometimes at the army office and sometimes at home. If I get well I will visit you at your army office, and if not, I can come to your house." After that, I did not get another chance to meet him again, and that was our last meeting.

On the eve of his death, he told my servant Buné that it was their last meeting. Buné said to me, "Strange! He came to me yesterday evening and told me such things." I asked him about his illness. He said, "There is nothing serious and he had a good appetite." I said, "It is doubtful. Isn't he about to die?" He said, "I don't think he will die, because he told me that he was fine." I added, "It is doubtful. Since he is quite different from others, it could mean that he was about to die." Buné replied that he wouldn't die.

The next when I looked for Buné, he was nowhere to be seen. I asked my wife if she had sent him somewhere to do a job, and she said she did not. Actually he had gone to Gendün Chöphel's house early in the morning. After a while, he came back with a gloomy face. I asked him what happened and where he had been. He said, "I went to the teacher's house. He is dead." I asked him if there were other people there and he replied that there was no one. I went to his house and asked his wife how he had died, and she replied, "He died this morning at sunrise. Before his death, he asked me to help him face eastward, though normally he faced south. So together we turned his face towards the east." Buné told me that when he entered his room, Gendün Chöphel was sitting erect with a pillow for back support. Some government officials of who were his disciples conducted the funeral. My servant was also there to help them. He told me that only Gendün Chöphel's wife was there during his last hours. They saw him say his final prayers before he died. He did not take any medicine.

Gendün Chöphel once told me that the Chinese army camp in Lhasa requested him to work for them and said that they would give him a salary. He said, "As I am very popular, the Chinese asked me to work for them and they told me that they would give me a salary. But I refused, saying that I spent many years in prison and had become mentally ill. I added that I was useless to anyone and would not be able to work." After he was released from prison, he did not do any work. I think his illness lasted for not more than a month and he passed away shortly after that.

NOTES

1. To put a black hat on a white person (mi dkar po la zhwa mo nag po g.yog pa) is a Tibetan proverb, meaning to put blame on an innocent person.
2. Hugh E. Richardson (1905–2000) was a British diplomat in Lhasa from 1936 to 1940 and again from 1946 to 1950, in the final years having become the diplomatic representative of the recently independent India. He was also a great Tibetologist. His academic work focused on the history of the Tibetan empire, and in particular on epigraphy After his retirement from public service he returned to St. Andrews and spent the remainder of his life as an independent scholar.
3. Chang is undistilled fermented liquor and beleived to less harmful than hard alcohol.
4. Golden beverage (usually chang and tea) offered to the gods for the success of a journey, enterprise, etc.

Recollections of Gendün Chöphel

Nangra Gendün Zöpa*

I heard from Gendün Chöphel himself and some people from his native region that he was born to a wealthy family at Shopang Lakha *(shong spang la kha)* in the Rebkong region of Amdo. His father was a Tantric practitioner. At a very young age, he was admitted to a small monastery in Rebkong called Tashikhyil, which had around sixty monks. He stayed there until he reached the age of about 16. After that he joined Dhitsa Monastery, a branch of Lamo Dechen Monastery *(la mo bde chen dgon pa)* and the seat of Zhamar Rinpoche. It had around 700 monks and taught epistemology and dialectics in their monastic course. He stayed there until he was in his twenties. There, he was called Dhitsa Alak. Amdo people call a lama "A-lak". He then joined Thösamling College of Tashi Gomang Monastery where he studied for seven or eight years. There he became very popular because of his natural aptitude for scriptural studies. However, that earned him the enmity and jealousy of other monks, forcing him to return to his former monastery Tashikhyil in Rebkong. He was welcomed back by the monks and was requested to stay there and look after the monastery. He wanted to join one of the [Three Big Geluk Monasteries in Lhasa][1], but he was not able to

---

* He was born in around 1906 in Tsongon Nangra in Amdo. At the age of fifteen, he came to Lhasa and took admission in Drepung Monastery. His monastic section (khangtsen) was Lubum. Since he and Gendün Chöphel were in the same monastic section, they became close friends. Later, when Gendün Chöphel was arrested and imprisoned, Nangra Gendün Zöpa was serving as section master and a teacher in the monastery. He made many efforts to effect Gendün Chöphel's release from the prison; after Gendün Chöphel's release, he arranged lodging and other facilities for him.

tell the monks about this, thinking that they would never allow him to leave the monastery, unless he said something really offensive to them. Therefore, at a meeting in the presence of the lamas and senior monks, he stood up and said, "You are all crows and I am a cuckoo bird; there is no reason for me to stay here." Greatly offended, the senior monks angrily spatted, "Let us be crows. If you are a cuckoo, then go wherever you like." He promptly left for Lhasa, riding horses or mules. He joined Drepung Monastery in Lhasa and his monastic section was Lubum House. This much is what I know about his birthplace.

There seems to have been a controversy surrounding the issue of whether he was the reincarnation of a Lama. From the time he was admitted to Dhitsa Monastery, he was known as "Alak Dhitsa." When at Tashi Gomang Monastery, he once made a paper toy boat, which when lit with a candle crossed the Sangchu River. He was not yet thirty at that time.

Drepung Monastery's section Lubum Khangtsen was known for its strict discipline. Popularly called the "Lubum of the East" and the "Tehor of the West," these two monastic sections had a reputation for their monastic discipline. I joined the monastery three years after Gendün Chöphel joined it. I was fifteen at that time. Because we belonged to the same monastic section, we knew each other well. It was during the time of the Thirteenth Dalai Lama. I do not know the year of Gendün Chöphel's birth, but he seemed to be no more than fifty when he died. While at the monastery, he proved to be excellent in the academic sphere as well as in discipline, so everyone at the monastery had great respect for him. He was hardly ever seen reading texts. Monks from our section used to say that he would not study the scriptures. He usually spent his time either drawing and painting or gossiping and playing with the junior monks.

In our monastic section, we had a geshe called Sernya *(gser nya)*, who was very audacious and funny. Gendün Chöphel used to carry a blue sheet to wrap and carry things whenever he went to Lhasa. He had many acquaintances among the aristocrats in Lhasa. He used to draw portraits of their children and received gifts in return. He also received regular pocket money from the monastery, which he used to cover his living expenses. Whenever he returned from a visit to Lhasa, he would put down his luggage and take a rest at the gate of his monastic section building, located in front of Geshe Sernya's quarter. Geshe Sernya would always ask him which aristocrat families he had visited, and what gifts he had received from them. Sometimes Gendün Chöphel returned empty-handed, but even if he had got nothing, he would tell the Geshe that he had made such and such drawings and received such and such gifts and money in return. Geshe Sernya would in turn him tell him jokingly that he would become rich very soon. Gendün Chöphel used to tease the Geshe.

One day, when he returned to his monastery from his visit to Lhasa, he filled his bag with stones near the gate and took a rest near Geshe Sernya's residence. The Geshe quickly came out from his room and asked Gendün Chöphel to show him the bag. He refused, but the Geshe snatched the bag and searched it. As there were only stones inside and nothing else, Geshe Sernya felt rather offended and angrily rebuked him, "You made fun of me, one who occupies the front seat in the assembly of Drepung Monastery. This is extremely bad. Let me take you to the Chief Proctor." Gendün Chöphel ran away and locked himself in his room. (Our monastic section had four common dormitories. The upper one was a four-storied building, located right above the main building of our monastic section. Gendün Chöphel lived in a middle room on the top floor. The room was relatively spacious and pleasant.) Geshe Sernya pushed the door, saying he would take him to the Chief Proctor. After many pleas, Gendün Chöphel was finally spared.

One sunny day, he went to visit an aristocratic family in Lhasa. Since it was scorching hot, he took a rest under the shade of the Zhöl pillar. As he sat down, he noticed ancient scripts on the four sides of the pillar. He realized the historical significance of the pillar. It was only then that he came to know about the existence of the inscription.

At that time he was studying in the Upper Class of Madhyamika or Middle-Way Philosophy *(dbu ma rnying pa)* at Gomang College. Monks from affiliated branch monasteries *(grwa rgyun)* were not required to attend classes on the study of Dialectics Based on Colour

Methods *(kha mdog dkar dmar)* and the study of Mind & Mental Factors and Basic Logic *(blo rigs rtags rigs)*. So like other monks from affiliated monasteries, Gendün Chöphel spent exactly seven years on the study of various topics of Buddhism, dedicating a year each to the Seventy-fold Factors *(don bdün bcu)*, the Lower Class *(gzhung 'og ma)*, the Upper Class *(gzhung gong ma)*, the first chapter of Abhisamayalamkara *(skabs dang po)*, the Perfection of Wisdom *(phar phyin)*, the Lower Middle-Way philosophy *(dbu ma gsar pa)* and the Upper Class of Madhyamika *(dbu ma rnying pa)*.

During a debate on the Middle-Way philosophy, two monks each from Loseling and Gomang colleges of Drepung Monastery were required to debate in the courtyard. From the Gomang side, we had Gendün Chöphel and another monk whose name I do not remember. Loseling was represented by Tehor Kyorpon and the other monk was Gyalrong Kyorpön (recitation teacher) or a monk who was wealthy and held the title of Kyorpön. Debates were held throughout the night, and tea was served to all the monks attending the debate. I was one of the tea servers. The whole debate ground was filled with monk spectators. A month or two after that debate Gendün Chöphel left the monastery.

We later heard that he had gone to India. People said that he was silly to leave the monastery and travel to India. However, the fact is that Geshe Sherab was the main reason for him leaving the monastery and travelling to India. Geshe Sherab was from our section. He was learned, yet very overbearing. He had more than two hundred monks who would come to listen to his interpretation of the Buddhist scriptures. After joining the monastery, Gendün Chöphel seems to have attended Geshe Sherab's class. However, he stopped attending the class after a month or two. One of the monk students asked, "Why do you prefer to confine yourself to the darkness of your small room instead of attending Geshe Sherab's teachings? Geshe will reprimand you." To this Gendün Chöphel replied, "Whatever he teaches, I already know. And he has nothing new to teach. So it doesn't make any difference to me whether I attend his class or not."

The monk student immediately reported this to Geshe Sherab, who angrily exclaimed, "This new student is saying such things?" Since he was a great Lama, he was quite arrogant and hot-headed. Even I admit that he was short tempered. Gendün Chöphel later told me that he was compelled to leave the monastery because he was always scolded.

When Geshe Sherab went to China with a Chinese official, he travelled through Calcutta. Gendün Chöphel was in Calcutta at that time. He later told me that he went to see Geshe Sherab and argued with him, saying, "You're a ruthless and jealous guy. You forced me to leave my monastery. I hear that you are going to China. Don't ever say that the earth is flat and so and so. These days, people from different parts of the world are travelling here and there. They have clearly seen how the earth appears. So it is better not to make a fool of yourself." Geshe Sherab did not get angry that time. He just said to his attendant, Kalsang, "Kalsang, Gendün Chöphel is saying such things to me."

Gendün Chöphel had created many mural paintings in his room. There were drawings of kittens fighting, birds flying in the sky and a skeletal-looking lama with many wrinkles and protruding bones and ribs, resembling the appearance of the Buddha during his famous six-months of austere practice. It was not portrait of a Tibetan Lama. He told me his name, but I don't remember it now. He had also created other murals in his house. He spent most of his time painting gods and deities or drawing pictures. At times, he would play or gossip with newcomers like me. He did not read or study scriptures very often. I can't tell if he did his study during the night hours. But I have seen him reading the scriptures before leaving for the debating ground.

His paintings looked more beautiful than photographs, so aristocratic families' children asked him to draw their portraits. Those who were thin would ask him to make them a little fatter. He would make their pictures as beautiful as they wanted. Pleased with the outcome, they would bestow gifts on him. He lived quite comfortably. Most of his paintings were in black and white. The birds drawn on his walls were painted in colours.

Gendün Chöphel told me that he learned English in just six months. While at the monastery, he was a very good monk. He was calm, friendly to everyone and good at his studies. Therefore all the students of the monastery used to regard him highly. He seemed to have disrobed in India. He told me that he studied English under a teacher, who was possibly a Ladakhi or a Kinnuari (Khunu). I was twenty-two or twenty-three then.

I was doing a small business at that time, so I went to Kalimpong. Gendün Chöphel was also there. I cannot recall what conversation we had at that time. Later, when he came to Lhasa, he narrated his Indian experiences to me.

> I roamed around the Indian plains. I only had a bag and a book with me. With only these two items, I roamed around the Indian plains for a while. One day I booked a ticket from Siliguri. When I went away and looked at the ticket, I found that the amount written on the ticket and I paid were different and the man had taken extra money from me. I returned to the ticket counter but I was denied entry. I questioned why I was not allowed to enter and why they took extra money from me. Immediately, they returned the additional money that they had taken from me.

> One day in Calcutta, a police constable and a thief conspired together and took away my bag and the book. I immediately went into a shop where there was a telephone. I inquired about the phone number of a nearby police station and the shop owner gave me the number. I called up the police station and reported that a police officer stationed at a particular area had taken both my bag and notebook at a certain time and place. I also asked for the identity of the police officer on the phone. He said they would come immediately. After some time, a team of high-level police officers arrived and we went to the police station. Within a short time, the police officer was brought in and my bag and notebook were returned. I was asked what penalty I thought should be given to the police officer. Since I had got my bag and the book back, I said it was okay even if he was not punished, and I left the police station.

> Once while travelling through the Indian plains, a school in one village was over for the day. One school kid asked me to give him my water, as he was thirsty. Another kid said it was not proper to drink the water as the water belonged to a Muslim. Another kid said it was okay to drink the water as there was no separate water for Muslims and it was all the water of India. Saying this, he drank the water. It made me laugh.

One day while I was roaming about, I felt thirsty. I went to a teashop. I placed my notebook on the table and drank a glass of tea. A foreigner came to the tea stall. He asked whether he could look at my book and I said okay. After having gone through it, he asked whether I would give the book to him. I said okay. He really took the book and left. I went after him asking where he was going with my book, and he returned it.

Gendün Chöphel told me that he had worked as a teacher either in Kinnuar or in Ladakh, where he taught *The Praises of Tara (sgrol ma)* and Daily Prayers *(chos spyod)* to the students. He composed the *Guide to Bodh Gaya (rdo rje gdan gyi gnas yig)* at the time. The fact that he stayed for twelve years in India was mentioned in his letter to his mother that he sent from Lhasa. The letter also states: "Even the regular breeze felt like flames. But I did not succumb to its heat. The best Vishnu temple is at a place close to Madras (old name for Chenai). I shall see if I can be of any service to the Buddhadharma." When I showed him the letter, he immediately seized it and put it into his pocket.

When he was in Kalimpong, he met Chensel Kunphel-la[2] and Bu Rabga[3], both of whom received money from the Kuomintang.[4] It seems that they gave Gendün Chöphel as much money as he needed. That is how they became friends. He said, "They told me that if I wanted I would get high salary *(phogs)* from the Kuomintang, but I refused, saying I will never take salary from the Kuomintang." At that time, Britain had seized Mön Tawang from Tibet. The Kuomintang had asked Chensel Kunphel-la and Bu Rabga to draw a map of the Tibetan area seized by the British and send it to them (the Kuomintang). This fact came to be known later after an investigation conducted by our monastic section.

When Chensel Kunphel and Bu Rabga requested Gendün Chöphel to do the job for them, he agreed because he had to go to Lhasa anyway. At that time, there was a wealthy Bhutanese man named Drukpa Drakshö *(brug pa drag shos)*[5] in Kalimpong. Through his help, he went through Bhutan. Drukpa Drakshö also provided mules and servants for him, and sent him to Mön Tawang via Bhutan. From Mön Tawang, he went straight to Lhasa. When he arrived in Lhasa, a man dressed in a checked *chupa* (Bhutanese national dress) and a *omosu* cap[6], with a long stick in his hand, arrived carrying all his luggage.

Geshe Palden Ludup *(dpal ldan klu grub)*, a senior monk from our monastic section, who was able, knowledgeable, soft-spoken and loyal to the section, said, "Gendün Chöphel has come. It is good. He will stay in the Khangtsen." In Jamyang Nub, there was a room that belonged to our section. He asked him to stay there. After two days, he suggested that we should find a room for Gendün Chöphel.

There was a three-storied building named Wangden Pelbar, owned by Kündeling, located in front of the police station at Gyabumgang. On the topmost floor, Geshe Palden had a small room, which he gave to Gendün Chöphel as his residence. Since Gendün Chöphel was a learned man, many aristocrats used to visit him. Those aristocrats seem to have provided him with whatever was necessary for his needs. In that room, he composed the *White Annals*. His sponsors during that time were Tethong and Horkang. Whether there were other sponsors, I do not know, nor did I ask him.

During that time, there were three of us staying together. All three of us belonged to the same hometown and monastic section. He used to set a time for our going to him, and if we arrived late, he would close the door and would not open it even if we knocked. If we arrived at the set time, he would give us money and ask us to purchase particular items from the market. After we had eaten, he would say that he had work to do. He would smoke. He would not let us touch even the butts of his cigarettes, on which he had noted numbers and letters. This he would do quite often.

One morning, he told me that he was going to the Rama Gang. He said that there was a pillar there, and he wanted to examine its inscription. He left early in the morning and returned very late that day. He later remarked, "That was a new pillar. It doesn't have anything special on it. There is one at Samyé, which I must go and check." I don't know if he ever went there. He also told me that he had had great difficulty reading the stone inscription that was hidden amongst the bushes near the willow tree at the Jokang temple. He said that all the edges of the pillar and the letters on it had been chipped.

One day while he was writing a history of Tibet, he said he was going to Russia after he finished writing. I asked him why he was going to Russia. "Isn't it better to go to America instead?" He replied, "There are many educated people in Russia, but not in America. I want to let the whole world know that there is a Tibetan man like me in this world. I have no other reason than this."

He drew a map (of Mön Tawang) and sent it to Chensel Künphel and Bu Rabga. Later he would lament that because of them he had suffered greatly. They in turn sent the map in an envelope to the Kuomintang. When the British government of India discovered that both these men were Chinese spies, they opened the envelope and found the map. We came to know this fact after our monastic section made an inquiry about this. After that Chensel Künphel and Bu Rabga were sent to China.

The British told the Tibetan government that Gendün Chöphel was a communist, that his party's mission had not finished, and that when they had finished their plan, they would turn everything upside down. We later found that the British did this to attack Gendün Chöphel. As a result, the Tibetan government arraigned Gendün Chöphel for counterfeiting currency notes and finally arrested him.

When we inquired about his imprisonment, we were told that he was charged for circulating forged Tibetan 100-rupee notes. We wondered how a man who was not fond of money had produced forged money. First, he was held in Nangtseshak prison. Then Nangtseshak handed him over to the office, which I think was the Foreign Affairs Bureau, located on the top floor of the government's storehouse. There he was given fifty floggings. He was then transferred to the Zhöl office, where he remained for three years. Our monastic section could do nothing, except to make continuous inquiries about his condition for a year. Until the end, we wondered how serious the charges actually were.

Kashöpa was then a cabinet minister. Having received a letter of summons from the Kashak, Palden Ludup and I went to see them. They told us to submit a letter appealing for Gendün Chöphel's release, through the Kashak. Kashöpa dictated to us what we must include in the petition. We then submitted a petition, the gist of which read,

"Gendün Chöphel has become sick in prison and we appeal to the government to release him on a medical parole, and we will return him immediately without delay whenever instructed by the government."

We were required to visit the cabinet ministers or kalons at their private residences. Shatra was one of the cabinet ministers. During the visits, we had to carry money with us. Our petition needed to reach the Regent, so we had to meet his manager. The appeal was referred back and forth between the Regent and the Kashak three or four times. Finally, Gendün Chöphel's case was handed over to the committee of düngtsi officials. The meeting hall was situated above the Labrang Teng. I think there were only four senior secretaries *(drungyigchenmo)*—Chokteng, Gyabumgang, Bumtang and Tsemönling—and three Finance Ministers *(tsipön)*—Lukang, Namseling and Ngabö. We had to appear before them almost every day. After one and a half years, we two managed to have him released.

When we went to the drungtsi committee, we were always required to appear at the entrance of the office, where the meetings were held. At the door were a useless staff member of the Tse Office and a stupid *drungkhor* member of staff. We were given tea and lunch there. There was a thick-cushioned seat near the door and we would sit there throughout the day. Although we were allowed inside only once a month, our daily appearance was still considered strictly mandatory. When we failed to appear, they would reprimand us harshly saying, "Why didn't you come? Why are you people provoking us?" Whenever the officials passed between us, we had to stand up and bow down low. It seemed as if they were scrutinizing our attendance and us as well. It was not just the two of us; there were also many other people. This was their custom. In this way, we appeared at the office for many months. On some days, they would notify us that there was no office and that we did not need to come. Whenever we approached the *drung-tsi* committee, we had to carry a scarf and an envelope containing 25 *srang* money each as presents for the two reception staff. We had to ask them when we should come and they would tell us when we should come again. We mostly sat from 10 am to 2 pm and sometimes up to 3 or 4 pm when the office closed. We had to spend the whole day in this way. During the evenings, we would seek appointments at their private residences. We had to give them two or three tea bricks and an envelope with 50 *srang* money. We needed to place the envelope at one end of a scarf with the label facing towards the recipient and the scarf had to be stretched out. If we offered them sacks of rice or wheat, their servants would take them to their houses after showing the things to their masters from the door.

The ministers said that they would try to help Gendün Chöphel as much as possible, and that they would never do him any harm. They only said a few words. When the ministers returned the gifts to us saying they could not accept any money from a monastic section, we would plead with them to accept the money and we would leave it, as usual, at a place they were unable to reach. Then they would say, "Ok, as you wish." That was how they used to take the money. Some of them, when money was left on the table, would not even look at it; they would take it without any hesitation. Lukangpa did not take even a dented coin from our hands. I wondered if there was any aristocrat official who was as kind as him.

One day the drung-tsi committee said, "Tomorrow, he will be handed over to you two. You must bring a businessman who has a shop in Lhasa as a guarantor." There was a businessman named Zhölma Aku, who was from Silling (Xinning). He was from our monastic section and had a shop at Gyabumgang. We took him with us to the Kashak.. The ministers had brought Gendün Chöphel, accompanied by the treasurer and caretaker of Nangtseshak office. They called us inside. Gen Palden Ludup, Gendün Chöphel, Zhölma Aku and I went to the meeting. We were ordered to kneel down before them. First, the chief official among them said a few words. Then Lukangpa read out the text of a bond that was almost half the size of a sheet of Tibetan handmade paper *(bod shog)*. It contained everything we had written in our petition, including our statement, "We promise not to let him flee or disappear and will return him, without delay, whenever the government orders." After reading it, he put a seal on it. We put the seal of our monastic section on it. Then Palden Ludup, Zhölma Aku and I respectively put our own signatures on it. After that, they called out to the treasurer of Nangtseshak to come up. As he came up, they ordered him to open the seal of the door of Gendün Chöphel's house and to hand over the things properly to us. After that, the treasurer and some prison guards took us to the Kündeling's residence, Wangden Pelbar, where Gendün Chöphel had written the *White Annals*. He opened the seal of the door and handed over the house to us. The Nangtseshak's treasurer looked a bit hesitant; he might have been afraid, thinking that we would say that something was missing. When we entered the house, as it had been closed for three years, we found that all the furnishings - the two pairs of cushions, two mattresses, one table and blankets— had been damaged by insects and reduced to powder, so that there was nothing that we could touch. There were only one or two cooking utensils left, and nothing else. There was no altar or box. The two of us pretended that nothing was wrong, and told them that everything was all right. They felt happy about this.

Gendün Chöphel took something from the top of the pillar of the house and put it into the pouch in his *chupa*. I did not know what it was. He gave me the key. I locked the house and took him to my house. Sitting on a mattress, he took out an amulet from his pouch and put it on a table. That was his wooden amulet inside which he had kept a statue of Buddha Shakyamuni *(rdo gdan ma)* that was about one *tho*[7] measures in height. We chatted and joked for a while. During the meal, he told me that his wife would be coming. I said, "Do you have a wife?" He said, "Yes, I have a wife. She is very kind to me. In prison, I was not allowed to go outside but she could go outside. I used to send letters through her to some aristocrats and they would give me whatever I needed. She would go and bring them to me. My wife was very kind to me during my stay in prison." I knew that there were some prisoners who were allowed to go outside in the daytime but had to sleep in the prison at night.

In the evening just before dusk, she came carrying many filthy wrapped packages. Except for some things that she required, I kept the rest of her things in the storeroom. The woman looked very untidy. I was told that she was from Kham Nangchen. She was around twenty-five years old and clad in fur clothes. So this is the way we lived then.

One day, it was Ganden Ngachö, the anniversary of the death of Tsongkapa *(dga' ldan lnga mchod)*. On this occasion, people offer butter lamps and burn incense on the roof of their houses and recite "Aiming at Loving Kindness *(dmigs brtse ma)*". Gendün Chöphel said, "Today I want to go upstairs and look at the view." I said, "Yes, that's all right." He and his wife went upstairs, and did not come down for a long time. Many new monks from my monastic section came to my house, as they usually did. So, I told one of them to go and call Gendün Chöphel to have *thukpa* (Tibetan soup). He went up and came down immediately. He told us that Gendün Chöphel was crying. I wondered why he was crying. Finally, he came down. I told him, "Gendün, have a seat. The *thukpa* has got cold. You have come too late". As he sat on the mattress, he said, "The Lama Tsongkapa—what wonderful qualities, deeds and power he had!" and started crying. We all kept silent. After a while, we had our thukpa.

Then one day he said, "If Lord Tsongkapa had not appeared in Tibet, there would be no Tibetans now. We would have dispersed everywhere. Owing to the kindness of Tsongkapa, the Dharma has united the patriotism of our people. He invented the system of wood block printing, and since then there have been no changes in the Tibetan language and script." We used to listen to him whenever he spoke on important topics, but none of us ever thought of keeping his words in our minds, because we were ignorant. One day, he said, "The communist Chinese will surely come to Tibet." I asked, "What will they do when they come here?" He replied, "They will not allow you to live according to your wishes." I asked, "So, should we obey them and do whatever they tell us?" "Yes, you will have to obey," he said. I do not remember what other things he said at that time.

There was a man called Lobsang who lived near my house. During my absence, Gendün Chöphel would go to his house. One evening, Lobzang came to my house and said to me, "Today Gendün Chöphel told me that if the Chinese came, His Holiness would not be able to escape. If he could manage to escape later on, it would be very good."

Gendün Chöphel stayed in my house for two or three months. Then one day Gen Palden Ludup found a room near the gate of Lubuk.

He said to me, "You are a businessman. Gendün Chöphel could stay in that house." He asked Gendün Chöphel to move there. The house was not in good condition and was a little dark. After staying there for two or three days, he said that he did not like to stay there because the room was not good. Then, Gen Palden got a room on the middle floor of the Wangdü Khangsar house, which belonged to Sera Jé College. Both Gendün Chöphel and his wife moved into that house. The house was nice and they stayed there for a short while. I do not know what he did during his stay there. After his release from the prison, he said to me several times, "I, Gendün Chöphel, will serve no purpose." He had started drinking by that time. Soon after that, while he was staying in Wangdü Khangsar, the Regent Taktra's manager came and asked him to come to the Regent's large newly built house[8]. He stayed there for about two months. One day he came to me. He had stopped drinking at that time and had changed into a fine person. I asked him why the Regent had sent his treasurer to summon him. He said, "He has built a large new house and he asked me to write many auspicious lines in *Lan-tsa* script on the wall above the doors; so I wrote them." I said, "Now, you should not drink alcohol. It is not good for you if you drink." He said, "Yes, yes." However, he started again after that.

Around that time, one of my relatives from Kalimpong came to see me. He was a very frank man and did not keep secrets. He was straightforward and impetuous. Gendün Chöphel liked such people. He would listen to whatever he said. One day, my relative said to Gendün Chöphel, "Your wife is very filthy. What will you do with such a woman? Send her away or send her back to her home." Gendün Chöphel did send his wife to her native land, but I do not know whether he took the advice of my relative or did it of his own free will. He gave everything he had to her and sent her away. It happened while they were staying in Wangdü Khangsar. He gave her around 200 *dotsé* money and some other things.

Afterwards, Kashöpa asked him to live in his house. He gave him a room on the western side of his premises. We carried his mattress and table to that house. There was a boy in his house, but I do not know whether he was Kashöpa's son or not. He was well versed in

English. Gendün Chöphel told me that he taught the boy Sanskrit at his request.

One day I found an old woman staying with him as his wife. In the morning, on my relative's advice, he would give her some money and send her to buy rations. Then the two men would roam and while away the time in an alehouse *(chang khang)*. When she came back, finding the door locked, she would sit near the door for the whole day. He used to do such things.

In Kalimpong there was a man who lived in Chokpa Kothi; he was from the same monastery where Gendün Chöphel had studied. He had a gun. We also had guns and long swords. Gendün Chöphel, my relative and this man would always go to the riverbank carrying guns and drinks. On the riverbank, they would prop up a flat stone, draw a black circle on it, and shoot at it. If the shot hit the target, they would shout and drink. They did the same thing for many days. When it was Gendün Chöphel's turn to shoot, as he was unable to use the gun, he would ask his two companions to shoot. One day, when they were coming back and passing near the Tsarong residence, not far from my house, Gendün Chöphel insisted that he would carry the guns. Carrying the guns and slinging the sword at his waist, he staggered drunkenly towards our house. Some Tibetan *Tsedrung* officials were passing nearby and when they recognized him, they asked what he was doing. He gave a laugh, jumped into the air, raised the sword up, and ran away. After a while, he said to his friends, "Remove all these dirty things. I feel ashamed. Please take away the guns and the sword." His character was like that. He would also say, "We Amdo people will fight the Chinese like this." Sometimes, he would say, "If we fight against the Chinese, we will be not able to withstand them. They are extremely tough. If the Chinese come to Lhasa, they will transform it into an unrecognizable place."

One day when he was staying in Kashöpa's house, I said to him, "Gen-la, I am going to Kalimpong tomorrow." I was alone at my house, as I had already sent my relative back to Kalimpong. The next day, early in the morning just before sunrise, he came to my house. He said, "Are you going to Kalimpong today?" I said, "Yes, I am leaving now after having tea. I want to go on a pilgrimage. Have some tea." He said, "Give me a little alcohol." His hands were shaking because he used to drink regularly. Then he said, "One should drink alcohol in this manner" and sipped it slowly (his lips making a characteristic sound). After finishing the drink, his body would stop shaking. He always did that. He might have owed me around 12 or 13 *dotsé* money. "I cannot return your money," he said. "You can give it to me after you die," I answered. "Who will give it to you after I die? Since you are leaving today, we should celebrate." Saying this, he took out a scarf and put it around my neck. I said, "I have gone to Kalimpong many times before, but you have never offered me a scarf before—why did you offer me one this time?" He explained, "This is just a celebration between you and me, nothing else." I said, "Today I am going to visit holy places. I shall offer this scarf to the statue of Buddha Shakyamuni (Jowo Rinpoche)." He thought for a while and said, "Do not offer this to Jowo Rinpoche." I asked, "Then to whom should I offer it." He responded, "There is O Rinpoche on the top, offer this to him." I said, "Your father was a Nyingma practitioner. That is why you want to do this. I will not offer this to him. I will offer it to Jowo Rinpoche." With a laugh, he said, "It does not matter."

After this, I went to Kalimpong and stayed there for just over a year. In Lhasa, I had a friend called Lobzang Gyatso through whom Gendün Chöphel took money from me and gave money back to me. One day I suddenly remembered Gendün Chöphel. I thought, "He has no money. If I send a letter to Lobzang Gyatso telling him to give money to Gendün Chöphel, it will take many days." So I sent a telegram asking him to give any amount of money to Gendün Chöphel that he needed. After three days, I received a telegram saying that Gendün Chöphel had passed away the day before. "He was young and might have just reached fifty. It was a great tragedy," I thought. I returned to Lhasa. Gen Palden Ludup was weeping. When I asked him about the funeral rites and the holy body of Gendün Chöphel, he said that it was not possible to bring his holy body to our monastic section; some aristocrats had taken care of it. He told me the name of the cemetery ground near Sera, probably it was Phabongka, where he was buried.

He told me that the aristocrats had done a very good job. When I heard this, I felt very happy. When I asked what Gendün Chöphel had told him before his death, he said, "I got a message that I must go to his house the next day and I agreed. Because of the ongoing construction of our monastic section's house in Lhasa market, I didn't get time to go and see him. He died that day." When I asked what the aristocrats had said after that, he told me that Gendün Chöphel had asked them several times to take a photo of him. I think his photograph was taken. Later, Gen Palden gave me a photo in which Gendün Chöphel's eyes were closed and I put that photo inside my shopping register and kept it in the drawer.

One aristocrat had told Gen Palden Ludup, "He (Gendün Chöphel) said that his body is not able to hold his knowledge. An aristocrat replied that such great Tibetan scholars had appeared in Tibet in earlier times." Gendün Chöphel said, "Oh, it is true?" and took his last breath."

Horkang Geshe, who was compiling a Tibetan dictionary *(dag yig)*, came to my house one day. He and Gendün Chöphel were close friends. He said, "Gendün Chöphel has already finished making woodblocks for the Songtsen Gampo's section of the Tibetan history. His manuscript on Trisong Deutsen is with me. You can buy planks and make woodblocks for it." When I asked how much it would cost, he said, "About 200 *dotsé*s." I replied, "200 *dotsé*s is not a problem. However, making an order for planks in Kongpo, bringing them here, writing on the plank, then sculpting and printing—all these tasks are not for a businessman like me. I cannot do that." I was really very unfortunate, ignorant and useless. I could have taken the manuscript and printed it at Tharchin Babu's press or at the Mani Printing House in Kalimpong. Such an idea did not cross my mind as it was shrouded in darkness at that time. Later, I lost his photo that I had kept in my drawer and also the manuscript of the Songtsen history. By that time, the Chinese had already entered Tibet. Gendün Chöphel passed away after the Chinese entered Tibet. I heard that the Chinese had offered to buy these kinds of manuscripts for 10 Chinese *da-yang* money and they were planning to collect them, which I believe was true. Many new monks from my monastic section used to come to my home. I suspected one of them took the photo and the manuscript and sold them to the Chinese.

Gendün Chöphel passed away in 1951, didn't he? This year is 1979, and that means twenty-nine years have passed since then. The history of Songtsen had about seventy pages. He had written it in old Tibetan, and had written the meaning in modern Tibetan beneath each line. He wrote it before his arrest.

One day during his stay in Kashöpa's house, Gendün Chöphel was summoned to the Tse Office. He was given 60 *'bo* measures of grain, 4 *khal* measures of butter, 3 or 4 *dotsé* money and 3 or 4 teacakes. There was a four-storied building behind the building which I think was called Garushak, near the utensil store in the teaching courtyard. He was alloted a room in that building as his residence. The Agriculture Department was also in the Garushak building. He told them that he would continue with his history writing. I have no idea if he completed his work in that house or not. From Kashöpa's house he moved to that room, where he passed away.

When he was in India, the British government had put restrictions on his movements in India. I heard that while in Darjeeling, he received an invitation from a foreign country. He applied for and got a visa but as he was getting ready to leave, his passport was seized just a day before his departure, and he was denied permission. I think it was true. He travelled to Sri Lanka but he was not allowed to go to any other country.

At the time of his arrest, I think the chief security official of Nangtseshak *(mi dpon)* was Kungo Tashi Pelbar. The two of us went to him carrying a lump of meat. Kalön Rampa, Kashöpa and Zurkangpa were cabinet ministers at that time. They told us nothing else, except that they would do their best. Rampa said to us, "I will neither help nor harm in Gendün Chöphel's case." They would accept any money that we offered. Kashöpa was our advisor.

Zurkang one day gave us a severe reprimand. He was young at that time. I do not know if he did so out of dislike for Gendün Chöphel. We two went to him early one morning. He was washing his feet in a tub *(tong pan)*. I do not remember exactly what he said, but he made some offensive remarks to us. We had to go to them again after Gendün Chöphel's release from prison to express our gratitude. We also had to go to each of the *drung-tsi* officials - four senior secretaries *(drung yig chen mo)* and four heads of the finance department *(rtis dpon)* to present thank-you gifts. Most probably, we had offered a 100 *srang* money to each of them, except Lukangpa, who did not receive money. We bought two cans of toffees and persuaded him to accept them; he accepted them saying, "I have many children, and they can be given as presents to them." Except for that, he did not accept even a scarf from us. We went to the senior secretary of Gyabumgang, from whom we got to know that the British did all this to harm Gendün Chöphel. He said, "Two nations have talked to each other. I would not care about one individual. One person does not matter. He has already been freed." We realized that what he had heard before and what he said to us now tallied. No other aristocrats told us about this.

For a long time before the arrest of Gendün Chöphel many counterfeit Tibetan 100 rupee notes had been in circulation, and he was blamed for this and arrested. They found the accusation that he was a communist a preferable charge against him. Later, when they realized that he was not a communist, and that he was a learned man, they released him. If they had not known that, they would never have released him. Lukangpa was somewhat lenient to him. At first, he looked harsh and did not speak to us in a proper manner. Afterwards, he showed a somewhat positive attitude towards Gendün Chöphel. He invited him to his house soon after his release. Chöphel later told me about their conversation. Lukangpa had said to him, "Earlier the people of Golok fought a war against Silling. The central government did not help them with even 500 shotguns—the central government works like this. Had the government aided them, how helpful it might have been to them. This is how the government works."

I did not see the conditions in which Gendün Chöphel lived in Zhöl prison. I went there to give him food two or three times. He had been put into an underground cell. There was a ladder which had been pulled up. To call him up, the ladder had to be sent down and he would climb up the ladder. The prison guard was formerly a prisoner who had been caught scraping the layers of the golden sepultures where the holy bodies of the Dalai Lamas were enshrined. He lived on the upper floor in a very poor room. What we had to do with Gendün Chöphel, talking, giving, receiving, and so on, we had to do near the guard's room. We also had to give something to the prison guard, or else it was difficult for us to meet him. I think there were many cells underground. There was a small lawn on the prison premises. In prison Gendün Chöphel had a friend—I am not sure if he was Tsenya Lama from Sera Monastery. Gendün Chöphel, his wife and his friend were living together. This was the reason why he said his wife was very kind to him. In prison it was impossible to read and teach scriptures. Some aristocrats sent food to him, but considering their ego, they would not visit the prison as the place was so dirty.

Regarding his wife, he had a wife who was from Kham Nangchen. She was arrested and imprisoned by the police for fighting with the beggars who lived behind the Potala Palace and Zhöl village. She remained in prison, as she had no one who would bail her out. Later, when he was staying in Khashöpa's house, he had another wife, and she was by his side at the time of his death. I do not know her name but she was from Lhasa and was around forty.

Gendün Chöphel seemed to be fifty when he died. He was much older than me. I was perhaps 32 at that time. He would never speak to us about religion but instead he used to talk about important issues concerning the country. After his release, the lama (Taktra Rinpoche) of Dorje Drak monastery visited him several times. He was the one who published the *An Ornament to the Nagarjuna's Intent*. Tethong Rakra Rinpoche also came to see him very often. Some aristocrats also used to visit him, but I did not know who they were. His main patron was probably Sonam Topjor, the son of Rakra Tethong Rinpoche's elder brother. One day, some girls—probably Tethong's daughters—came to his house and told him that they did not know what knowledge was and they did not want to gain it. Gendün Chöphel walked in front of them, saying "You walk in a pretentious manner, you should walk like this." He would talk of dirty things only when he was asked, otherwise he would not speak about dirty things. I never heard him saying prayers.

Gendün Chöphel was extremely distressed over his imprisonment. He said to me several times, "Now, Gendün Chöphel will be useless." He said the same to me even after his release. I think he must have died in great emotional distress. When he came out of prison, he had not started drinking. He started drinking later and his hands started shaking. When he was at Regent Taktra's house, he did not drink.

Early one morning he came to my house. I said to him, "I started my business in order to save as much money as I can, but I cannot save money. Where does the main problem lie?" He replied, "You should be stingy. You should control your money. Even if it is five paisa[9], you should treat it as money and save it, so that you can become rich (*paisa-wala*)[10]. Otherwise, there is no way to become rich."

Again, one morning, before sunrise, he came to my house. His hands were shaking. He asked me to give him a glass of alcohol, which I gave him. He said, "You must control your money, or else you will not able to save money." I wondered why he advised me thrice although I had only asked him once. After that, one day he came to my house and asked me to accompany him to the Barkor market. I went with him. An old woman was making and selling *sha bag leb* (meat burger fried in oil) near the Sha Keyring *(shar skye ring)* flagpole. He went and sat near her and said to me, "Her meat burger is very tasty. I want to eat one." I suggested, "Let us buy some and eat them at home." He refused saying, "No, I will eat here." I got angry, thinking "Why is he eating on the road side of the Barkor?" and went home. He came back after a while and said to me, "It was tasty". I asked, "Why were you eating on the road side?" and he replied, "There is no difference between eating food at home and outside."

When walking on a road, he would never walk in the middle of the road. He would always keep on the right side of the road. When I asked him the reason, he said, "I walk slowly. So it is not good for those who are in a hurry."

When he was working on his history book, he was fine, and if we knocked at his door, he would never open it. He would open the door and come out only when he had finished his work for the day.

He could judge a person just by looking at his or her face. He described one of his friends, "I have a friend named Gyaji. If he were told to go straight along the way, he would never do that. He will not go straight along the way, even for distance of a half a day. He is one of those who will always do things the opposite way." He would tell us such funny things.

He did not care much about money. If he got money from an aristocrat, he would promptly go and buy meat, butter, etc., whatever he liked—he would use it immediately. He did not have the habit of saving money and being stingy. He did not have a single fine set of clothes. I gave him a shirt made from fur. He would wear a long poor quality *chupa* (traditional Tibetan dress). He had a pair of long boots with high heels made in Russia, and he would proudly say, "Mine are Russian shoes. They are good." They were old. If he had no work, he would sleep.

He had no possessions except for a statue of the *rdor gdan ma* (epithet of Buddha). He considered it a treasure, saying that it had been given to him by his father. He had put it in an engraved wooden amulet. He never made offerings of butter lamps or any other kind of offerings. He would sometimes visit places of worship, however.

When he was arrested, the government probably confiscated all his manuscripts and notes. Later, when I went to his residence, his books and other miscellaneous things were nowhere to be seen. He had a suitcase with a leather cover. Only his table was there. At the time of his death, that table was in front of him, as it appears in his photo. He never used to wear any new clothes. I am not sure if he had ever worn any new shirts.

I found that the Tibetan army's drill commands and other military words were in English language. Later, the Tibetan government commissioned Gendün Chöphel to translate them into Tibetan. When I asked him why they had been translated, he replied, "We have to speak in our own language. Why should we speak in another language? Our people pretend to know English, but their pronunciation is not good. If they say these words in front of foreigners, it will be a matter of shame."

Once he said to me, "If you want to find archaic Tibetan terms, you have to go to Mon *(glo yul)*. They say *na-si* for *nas*, and *ga-gro* for *gro*. All the old Tibetan terms are found Loyul and we cannot find them anywhere else."

Notes

1. Sera, Drepung and Ganden monasteries.
2. He was a favoured attendant of the 13th Dalai Lama, but some high Tibetan government officials framed charges against him and banished from Lhasa after the Dalai Lama's death.
3. He was a son of Pandatsang family from Kham.
4. After 1959, the Koumintang government of Taiwan started giving money to Tibetans to accept Tibet as part of China and to disseminate pro-Kuomintang and anti-Communist propaganda among Tibetan exiles. Many Tibetans were brainwashed by the money. Those Tibetans who received money were regarded as traitors by other Tibetans. The MTAC office is main agent that deals with the Tibetans in exile. The exile Tibetan government forbades all the Tibetans from contact the MTAC.
5. Drakshö *(drag shos)* refers to Bhutanese government official.
6. *o mo su* cap is a type of Monmouth cap.
7. The distance between the tip of thumb and the middle finger.
8. Gendün Chöphel was asked by Regent Taktra to make paintings at his newly built residence.
9. The smallest unit of Indian money; 100 paisa makes 1 rupee.
10. Paisa-wala is a Hindi term, which means "rich".

Gendün Chöphel in My Memory

Narkyi Ngawang Dhondup[*]

Regarding how I met Gendün Chöphel for the first time, it was when I was a student of Tsé School *(rtse slob grwa)*. The school's teacher usually came from Mindröling *(smin grol gling)*, and the name of our teacher at that time was Lodrö Chözang *(blo gros chos bzang)*. He used to teach at the school as well as at his home for those who wanted private tuition. He took us to meet Gendün Chöphel, who at that time was in prison. He had long hair and looked very untidy. As instructed by my teacher, I offered him a scarf and made prostrations to him. My mother had relatives in Dakpo, so I took a lump of butter cheese *(thud dar ma)* [from my home] and presented it to him. That is how I met him, accompanied by my teacher. The two had already discussed me before. So without any formalities, Gendün Chöphel simply said, "Oh! Is he the one?" "Yes, he is," my teacher replied. Then he quickly looked at my hands and said, "It is a little late, but it is good that we have met. Do not come here for the time being. It does not matter; we shall meet again later." He said nothing else. I also did not want to visit

---

[*] Born in Lhoka Tsethang in 1928, he was admitted to Drepung Monastery in 1935. In 1940 he joined the Tse School where he studied traditional Tibetan subjects. Through his Mindroling teacher, he got an opportunity to study with Gendün Chöphel for several years. He therefore knows details of his teacher. In 1952, he was sent by the Tibetan government to China to study. In 1958 was appointed as the caretaker of Lhasa Tsuklagkhang. In 1959 he came into exile in India. He served in the Department of Information and International Relations, the Library of Tibetan Works & Archives and other departments of the Tibetan Government-in-Exile in various capacities. He was a member of the committee for drafting the charter of the Tibetan Government-in-Exile and worked on the Tibetan typewriter project. He has contributed to the Tibetan struggle with dedication in various ways.

him at that time. I was there according my teacher's instructions; I did not know anything (about Gendün Chöphel) then.

The prison was at Zhöl Pangding. Since it was a prison, I did not feel comfortable there—I felt rather fearful and nervous. Nothing happened for about two years after that. Later when he was released from prison and was staying with Kashöpa, I went to see him with my teacher. My teacher requested him to give me tuition. My teacher then told me that I should learn Tibetan history from him and that I could study with him some new chapters on Tibetan history that were not in our course at that time. When Gendün Chöphel moved to the Department of Agriculture of the Tibetan government *(bsod names las khungs)*, my teacher told me that I could go to him to start my tuition. I went to his residence taking a lump of butter and a few teacakes as gifts—I went alone and my teacher was not with me. He said to me in jest, "You have to come to here every day." I replied, "I have already applied for a government job. I will come and see you, but how can I come every day?" I requested him to teach me history. He said, "I will think for a while." Then he told me a brief Tibetan history. He used to drink heavily. He always wrapped himself in a blanket, except when he went outside his home or upstairs. When teaching, he would give very clear explanations. At other times, he looked somewhat mentally ill. He was working on his book *White Annals*. He told me that he had a manuscript of it. It was yet to be printed at that time. He did not teach me anything on that day.

The next day, when I went to him after the morning tea session *(drung ja)*[1], he told me that he would teach me poetry. I had to listen to him. The first chapter of the poetry had no examples, so he just explained the meanings without giving examples, saying that we did not need them. He gave me a text and asked me to read the lines one by one. He explained each line as I read it aloud. He instructed me not to take any notes but to listen to him carefully. So I had to keep in my mind whatever he taught me. We quickly finished the first chapter. Though I went to him every day for a whole month, he only taught me occasionally. I was only able to go home late in the evening. He had many visitors every day. However, when I was with him, the only government staff who used to be in his house was Chicha-la *(spyi lcags lags)*. I had to wait for him to start the lessons. He used to tell us about various topics, such as Indian history, religious history, accounts of his visit to Sri Lanka, about British behaviour, Chinese behaviour and so forth. He advised me that I should go to China. He said that we must travel outside Tibet and know about what was happening in the outside world. He told me this on several occasions.

He used to recite the mantra of goddess Tara very often. He always asked me if I had any news to tell him. If I did not have any news to tell him, he would feel offended, so I always felt very worried. I studied with our Mindröling teacher, as well as with Kyilkhang Khen Rinpoche and Gen Peljor-la. He knew about this. When he asked me about what I had studied with them, I had to explain, like an oral test. It was uncertain whether there would be a class on any particular day. Sometimes as soon as I arrived at his house, he would ask me to open my textbook and he would start teaching. Not long after we finished the second chapter of the poetry text, including its examples, his health deteriorated and he passed away soon afterwards. That is the story of how I met Gendün Chöpel.

Some time before this, Rika Lobzang Tenzin once casually asked me questions about Gendün Chöpel, but he did not tell me he was writing a book about him. So, I just told him a few ad-lib comments on Gendün Chöpel without proper thought. Afterwards, he published a book with many errors. I did not know about this at first. Actually I had told him that when he was teaching, Gendün Chöpel always looked very lively. At times Gendün Chöpel would act if he was possessed by a deity. Sometimes, he would sing the Tara prayers and shed tears. He used to get up early in the morning. He would fix a time for me to come to him the next day. Sometimes he would ask me to be at his house early the next morning, and then if I went to him early the next day, he would keep me waiting. It was very difficult to judge. Sometimes, he would start the lesson suddenly on an impulse, and sometimes there was no tuition for almost a week. I used to go to him every day, but there was tution every day. I had to eat my lunch with him. I sometimes used to take food to him from home. I often supplied rations to his kitchen, but he did not know about that. I also had to provide alcohol for him. He never wore clothes. I gave him a few blankets one by one and he felt very happy. I had two blankets at my home in Tibet that had been used by Gendün Chöphel.

The chant-master of Gyutö Monastery, a tall fat monk called Minyak Kyorpön, occasionally visited Gendün Chöphel when I was with him. They used to talk mainly about Tantra and I did not understand their discussions. At times there were no visitors and only Gendün Chöphel and I were in the house. We used to eat our meal together. When I asked him any questions, he would give me short replies. Sometimes he would suddenly tell me, "Now you can go." Once I failed to go to him and the next day when I told him the reason, he reprimanded me sternly, thinking that I had taken leave without his permission. However, he never raised his hand to me. From then on, I went to him every day.

Sonam Topgyal, an official of Nangtseshak Office, who was my age, visited Gendün Chöphel frequently, although he did not learn anything from him; he was one of Gendün Chöphel's main patrons. When Gendün Chöphel died, he took upon himself all the main responsibilities pertaining to the funeral rites and kept his master's skull with him. Later, he went to China to study and finally became a teacher.

I was not at Gendün Chöphel's side at the time of his death. At that time, I had gone to the hot spring in Tölung (near Lhasa) with my relatives and some other people.

Gendün Chöphel believed in and practised all the Buddhist doctrines without discrimination. Sometimes some Nyingma lamas and practitioners would come to his house. They would perform a ritual. When I told him that it was a Nyingma ritual and I should leave, he would persuade me to stay. I had to stay, although I did not know anything about the ritual. At times, his house would be full of guests. There were sometimes around ten visitors at a time. He would recite prayers and suddenly he would shed tears. The chief lama among them, who was from Amdo, was in a monastic robe. Gojo Lachung Abo was a main patron as well as a student of Gendün

Chöphel. He used to meet Gendün Chöphel in prison and afterwards at his residence every now and then.

Gendün Chöphel would occasionally develop a sudden impulse to visit a place of worship. Whenever he went to the Jokhang temple, he would wear a *chupa*, but without proper style. I used to insist on modifying his way of wearing the *chupa*, or else he would dress carelessly. He had leather shoes with broad square fronts, which he wore rather awkwardly. He would ask me to accompany him. He would go straight to the statue of King Songtsen Gampo near the Barkor street. He would neither fold his hands in devotion nor would he recite any prayers before the statue. After a while, he would just sit outside for a long time like a tired pilgrim *(a jor ba)*[2]. After that, he would go down to the Jokhang. He did the same thing the following day. From the teaching courtyard to his house was only a short distance.

One day he told me to go to the Barkor market with him. I accompanied him. Dishevelled in his appearance, he looked exactly like a mad beggar. I was wearing a yellow shirt and the costume of the monk officials of the Tibetan government. Going down from Jowoi U-tra *(jo bo'i dbu skra)*, a willow tree near the Jokhang temple, passing through the front side of the Jetingling park *(bye sdings gling)*, then through the front side of the mandala of Manjushri, he went up to the Shasar Gang *(sha gsar sgang)* ground. There was a small stall where meat burgers *(sha bag leb)* were sold. He stood there for a while looking at it. Then he said, "Now let us eat meat burgers. They are tasty." I refused. He insisted and told me to sit down. There were many passers by there. It was the most embarrassing moment that I had ever experienced. When I hesitated, he said angrily, "Are you not going to sit down!" He nearly rebuked me. I felt obliged to sit down. The meat burger seller must have thought that he was an insane father. Then he gave me his half-eaten meat burger to eat. I didn't dare refuse; I ate it but I felt quite embarrassed. After that, we went around the Barkor market until we reached the Gyantsé shop, from where he turned back and entered the teaching ground through its main gate and looked at the murals. In the market, he bought a few things that he needed for which I paid. We arrived back at his home just before dusk. As soon as he sat down, he said to his wife, "Today, I embarrassed him. He felt ashamed. He, as a tsedrung official, is wearing a yellow shirt. I made him feel ashamed." I realized that he had done it to tease me. I said to him, "Please, do not do that sort of thing in future."

One spring evening he went up onto the roof of the building of the Agriculture Department to refresh himself. He would do this rarely, only once in a blue moon. The sun was about to set and the shops and stalls at Sabogang market had closed. As usual, people from Drib village (south of Lhasa) had come to the market for a while to sell *su-lu (*a type of incense) and other things. People would go there to buy these things. Gendün Chöphel said to me, "A few years from now, this kind of scene will disappear. People will not know anything about the Barkor; they will have no time to gather here."

He sometimes spoke to me very seriously, criticizing the mistakes of the Tibetan government and the people of Central Tibet *(dbus)*. He said, "You government officials say, "We are Lhasa people. We are the people of Central Tibet. You are *rojorwa (ro sbyor ba)* or *bangzen (sbang zan)*. "Bangzen" means one who eats the residue of brew *(sbang ma)*, and "rojorwa" means one who embalms corpses. In future, you people who call others "eaters of brew residue" will not even get brew residue to eat. Your corpse will have to be embalmed."

He continued, "The government officials are very stupid. They are engrossed in their own limited sphere. They are too busy competing among themselves to expand their estates and serfs. They even kill lamas. They must be open to the outside world; they must establish relations with foreign countries. Tibet cannot continue to exist if they do not keep in contact with the outside world. In the past, the snowy mountains could protect the country, but now they cannot. In the past, everyone had the freedom to profess their own religion, now it is not so. We must establish relations with other countries. It is very important that we have contact with India, China, the USSR and Germany."

He also mentioned the USA but did not specifically say that we should have relations with her.

He said that we must develop relations with the British, but he had a negative view of them. He strongly criticized the tradition of treating Central Tibet separately. He argued that the people from lower Tibet (Kham and Amdo) should be able to move freely to Central Tibet and people from Central Tibet should go down there. He had strong reservations about the Tibetan language as well. He said, "The Lhasa dialect is awful. They speak in a way which is different from the actual Tibetan phonology. We have to preserve our language through the script."

He had a metal box in which he had kept many loose (unbound) texts and manuscripts written in his own handwriting on white papers manufactured in Inida. He had a text called *bya len ma (Shakuntala)*[3], which was possibly not more than one hundred pages long.

He had a deep faith in deity Jetsun Tara. A skilled artist, he had drawn an image of her, painted light green with water colour. It was not very big. He used to keep it in different locations. Sometimes he would hang it on the pillar. Under it, he would put his own photo, which he had taken in India when he was young. He was not in monk's robes in that photo. There was another photo of him taken in Shillong. There were in total four photos of him. When staying in house, he would wrap himself up in a blanket and wear nothing else. He would smoke and drink very often.

Kashöpa's son used to come and see him sometimes. The son would say bad things to him, and he would say only bad things in return; they never talked nicely. The boy would not stay for long but would come often. Sometimes Gendün Chöphel would say, "Now he has come. Why have you come here? Go away." The boy would squabble, "You have no right to send me away. This is a government house. I will stay here." Gendün Chöphel usually took care of the boy, but did not teach him anything.

I did not hear anything from Gendün Chöphel about the circumstances that led to his arrest. The versions that I heard from Kashöpa and our Mindröling teacher Lobzang Chözang about his arrest were quite different. I first heard from the Mindröling teacher. According to him, while in Kalimpong, Gendün Chöphel published an article in which he expressed his views on the need of democratization of the Tibetan government, land reforms, reforms of the legal system and funding the monasteries to enable the monks to concentrate on their studies. My teacher said that the mastermind behind this was a Russian man, most probably Roerich, who believed in communist ideology. He further told me, "At that time, the British (in India) informed Richardson (British representative in Lhasa) that Gendün Chöphel was a communist and was associated with Russia and China. In Kalimpong Gendün Chöphel had a friend called Apo Rabga who worked for the Kuomintang, and had formerly acted against the Tibetan government. They had set up an association, and Gendün Chöphel helped him in drafting their memorandum, although he was not a member of that group. He went to Bhutan and prepared a map of the country". Richardson told Kashöpa all this and Kashöpa in turn reported it to the Kashak. The Kashak then ordered his arrest. [Rika] Lobzang Tenzin has said in his book (*The Life of Gendün Chöphel*) that Gendün Chöphel was arrested in Tsona but this is not true. When he returned to Tibet from India, he spent some time in Tsona, but his arrest took place in Lhasa.

On the morning of the day of his arrest, he went to meet the junior tutor of His Holiness the Dalai Lama. The junior tutor's bodyguard would normally be there. Gendün Chöphel had left his manuscripts with the junior tutor, but that morning he took them away. The officer who arrested him was Kungo Tashi Palrab. I was at school when the incident took place and did not know much about it—I just heard about it from others.

Later, when Kashöpa was in China to meet his children who were in a school in China, I served as his interpreter because I knew the Chinese language better than those who were already in China. At that time, I got an opportunity to ask him about the case of Gendün Chöphel. He told me that he had heard that Khunu Tharchin[4] sent a report (about Gendün Chöphel) to the government of India. Richardson then reported to the Kashak who in turn arrested Gendün Chöphel. However, he never said that he was in any way involved in this case. I don't know the facts. Gendün Chöphel certainly had contact with Khunu Tharchin. He had contact also with both [George] Roerich and Khunu Tharchin. When Roerich got some Dunhuang documents, he sought Gendün Chöphel's help to study the contents. Later using those documents, Gendün Chöphel composed the *White Annals*. I heard from Khunu Tharchin that he secretly studied Marxism under a woman friend of Roerich, Tharchin Babu told me that there was an Indian man in the Pomda's party and that he was not sure whether he remained a member of the party later. Because of his presence, the matter came to the notice of the government of India. According to Tharchin Babu, the logo and official documents of the party were designed by Gendün Chöphel. Their official letter pad with the logo was sent to Tharpa Press or some other big printing house in Calcutta for printing. The press sent an inquiry to Tharchin Babu in Kalimpong about the letter pad. The British were very meticulous. This was the cause of the issue. After that Tharchin Babu observed Gendün Chöphel and sent a report to the British government of India, which in turn informed Richardson about this. Gendün Chöphel made a map of Bhutan, and that increased the British mistrust towards him. They told the Tibetan government that he was working as a spy for Russia and that he was a communist. The British were not very suspicious about him being a communist but they suspected him of being a Russian spy.

Later, after his release from prison, Gendün Chöphel lived in Kashöpa's house. Kashöpa himself came to him morning and evening and prostrated before him and expressed his repentance. I saw him when he was in Kashöpa's house.

The Tsé Office proposed to the Kashak that they should ask Gendün Chöphel to complete his unfinished *White Annals* and give him a monthly salary. The Kashak issued the necessary instructions to Gendün Chöphel, and he was quite clear in his mind about the *White Annals*. He said that he would continue to work and make further additions. At that time, he mentioned a name of a document, but I did not know it exactly. When I recall it now, he might have mentioned the Dunhuang documents. He told me that he had many ancient manuscripts related to Buddhism but he was working mainly on history.

Dawa Zangpo[5] was also present at that time. He normally did not come when I was there. I do not know why—maybe because I was a government official. He would just come and then leave quickly.

Gendün Chöphel was very skilled at painting. He was very good at both classical and modern art, as well as the traditional style of thangka painting. He could draw my portrait just by looking at me and he did not take long to finish it. Sometimes he would draw the image of goddess Tara. I still have images of Tara and Indian Buddhist scholar Dandi done by him.

He knew English, Sanskrit, and also Hindi and Chinese. Two Hasak men, one was said to be a leader of Hasak, who had fled from Xinjiang, visited him a few times. They did not stay long in Lhasa. I saw them at Gendün Chöphel's house only once, but I heard that they visited him a few times. In their conversation, they spoke Tibetan occasionally but they talked mainly in another language that I did not understand. He spoke mainly about his work *Arts of Love Making*.

Half jokingly, he used to say that it was too bad to treat Central Tibet separately. He used to say, "We have to mix together. We, all the Amdo people, were from Central Tibet. You will not become a monk so you should marry an Amdo woman."

There are two versions regarding the circumstances of his death. Most people say that he had developed an excess of water in his body. I was not near him at the time of his death. Some said that he received medical treatment from a Chinese or a German doctor. Some told me that after the Chinese doctor gave him a few injections, his condition deteriorated and he died.

Notes

1. Drungja *(drung ja)* was a morning tea session held at Norbulingka attended by monk officials of the Tibetan government before 1959.
2. A pilgrim, carrying a long staff, who travels to different sacred places in Tibet.
3. Full name: *bya len ma mngon par shes pa'i zlos gar* (Shakuntala by Kalidas).
4. Gergan Tharchin was popularly known as Khunu Tharchin, Tharchin

Babu or Babu Tharchin among Tibetans.
5. Dawa Zangpo was a Japanese spy, who visited Tibet in the disguise of a Mongolian monk. His real name was Hisao Kumura. See his autobiography *Japanese Agent in Tibet,* London: Serindia Publications, 1990.

A REMINISCENCE ABOUT GENDÜN CHÖPHEL

*Alak Jampel from Choné**

I heard about Gendün Chöphel for the first time from Lobzang Yeshi, an official of Taklung Drak Monastery, who was at that time acting as a leader of the Amdo militia group based in Lhoka[1]. He knew Gendün Chöphel personally, because he used to learn history and other things from the latter. Tepo Pa Tsering *(the po pa tshe ring)*, who was from my native land, was a servant of Lobzang Yeshi. When I was at the monastery, everyone said that Gendün Chöphel was non-Buddhist. Because of that I got the impression that Gendün Chöphel was not a good person who deserved respect, although I had never seen him.

One day when I went to meet Pa Tsering at his house, Gendün Chöphel was there. Pa Tsering said, "It is so good that two lamas have come here today. Please, both of you Rinpoches make yourselves comfortable. I shall prepare a meal for you." He introduced Gendün Chöphel to me and then he introduced me to him, saying, "This is Chepa Alak; he is from my native land." Gendün Chöphel asked me about my native land and I replied that I was from Sewarong *(se bo rong)*, lower Choné *(co ne)*, ." He then moved on to topics such as the life stories of the Buddha. However, since I had heard that he was

---

* He is the Chukar Trulku, a brother of Trulku Chunag Lungpa of Tagtshang Lhamo. He was born in Chone area in Thebo. He lived in Labrang Monastery for a long time. Later he came to Drepung Monastery, where he became close to Gendün Chöphel. He came to India before 1959 and lived in Kalimpong. Afterward he joined in Education Department [of exiled Tibetan Government] and carried out educational tours and related works for many years. Because of offering great service for the Department of Education, Dharamsala, he came to be known as Sherig Alag (Rinpoche of Department of Education).

non-Buddhist, I asked him to speak on any other topic apart from Buddhism. This is how I met Gendün Chöphel for the first time, through Pa Tsering. I met him several times after that, also through Pa Tsering.

Gendün Chöphel told me that I must visit his house. So one day I paid a short visit to his house. In this way, I got to know him. Initially, I was not sure if he was non-Buddhist, but he seemed to be sceptical about Buddhism.

During his last days, in a despondent mood, he sometimes recited the following four lines of the prayer of goddess Tara in a very melancholic tone:

> phyag 'tshal rab tu dga' ba rgyas pa'i//
> dbu rgyan 'od kyi phreng ba spel ma//
> bzhad pa rab bzhad tu ta ra yis//
> bdud dang 'jig rten dbang du mdzad ma//
>
> (Homage, Joyful Mother,
> Whose brilliant diadem spreads out garlands of light.
> With mocking and laughing TU TA RA,
> Subjugating Mara and the world.)

He used to recite only these four lines. When he recited these, he would insist that everyone around him, including his students and his wife, should recite them along with him. If others did not recite these in tune, he would feel offended and rebuke us. It seemed that when he was in prison he used to sing these lines and shed tears. When he finished the prayer, he would say, "OK, it is like this! The one who released me from prison was the Goddess Tara." I then thought that he had not lost his faith in Buddhism, because he would not believe in Tara if he had no faith in Buddhism.

He had a scroll painting of Syamatara, a green Tara with four hands, holding a sword in one hand. After his death, most of his manuscripts and notes were taken away by Horkhang's son. So I am almost sure that the painting was also taken by Horkhang's son. There was a text of Syamatara translated by Gendün Chöphel; I think because of that he was called Lotsawa. Since Syamatara is also a form of Tara, he clearly had a deep faith in the deity.

It was perhaps in the beginning of 1952—Chinese troops had already arrived in Tibet—he used to wrap himself in a red blanket that I had given to him and sit leaning against the wall. At that time he was not suffering from any particular illness. Except for the blanket, he wore nothing, neither shirt nor pants. When he went to the toilet, he would pull up the blanket awkwardly, its ends grazing the ground. If he did not drink alcohol, his head and hands would shake. He would ask especially for me to bring him alcohol, saying that we were the same Amdo people. After I gave him alcohol, he would drink and remain silent and motionless for a few minutes. He would then lean against the wall and rest, as if he was a bit tired.

One day he was drunk and resting against the wall, motionless as if he was asleep. I did not say anything to him because I thought he was sleeping. After a while, he woke up and said, "Oh! Oh! How pleasant a place it was! How beautiful it was! It was the entrance to the Fortunate Realm. How happy will I be if I really get there! Oh! Oh! How beautiful the flowers were! How pleasant it was! I wish I could visit that place!" At that time, two doubts arose in my mind: either this was a sign that he was going to die or it was just a fake *sadhana* (meditative accomplishment). However, by that time my doubt that he was a non-Buddhist or a heretic had already gone. After that, his health collapsed and he was ill for about two months. I promised him that I would go to meet him whenever I happened to visit Lhasa. He said, "It is very difficult for me to meet people from my native land. Even if I meet a few, they are generally of no use. You are a good person." He liked me very much.

Later, when I went to Lhasa, he was in very poor health. His body had swollen up like an inflated balloon and his limbs had become thin. The medicines did not help. Finally, Sonam Topgyal, the secretary of the Nangtseshak office, who visited him regularly since his days in prison, allotted a room on the top floor of the Garushak building to his residence, and assigned him to complete his history book *White Annals*. He was also given a monthly salary in the form of cash or grain, besides other facilities. I think Sonam Topgyal had promised to help him, because he used to come to Gendün Chöphel's quarters after office hours every day, although he did not learn anything from him. When the students gathered and sat in a circle, he would sit on a chair. A kettle containing *chang* (Tibetan brew) would be placed on the table in front of him. He would drink heavily and his face would turn red. Although he called himself a student of Gendün Chöphel, he never studied with him. He was seen with Gendün Chöphel most of the time, but I did not know whether he was doing so for his own purposes or for some other reason.

Around that time, a Chinese dance troupe came to Tibet. The group had a boy named Fanjoi. He and an old Muslim man called Wumari from Yuwaling, the Muslim camp in Lhasa, became friends through their interest in music and dance. Through Wumari, Sonam Topgyal met Fanjoi and they became friends. Sonam Topgyal might have discussed with Fanjoi the treatment of Gendün Chöphel. Fanjoi brought along a Chinese doctor, who gave Gendün Chöphel injections four times a day. Gendün Chöphel's condition deteriorated and he passed away. This is how he died. However, it is very difficult to say whether he died because his lifespan was exhausted or due to the strong injections given by the Chinese doctor, as we have no direct evidence. I was present when the doctor gave him injections. The doctor was from the Chinese dispensary located near Lubuk in Lhasa. Whether his lifespan finished or the Chinese malevolently harmed him, whatever the case may be, the most important thing is that the Tibetan government did not do the slightest harm, not even as tiny as a sesame seed, to Gendün Chöphel.

Later, one day when we were chatting near the banks of the Yamuna River, close to Ladakh Buddha Vihar in Delhi, Lobzang Tenzin asked me for information about Gendün Chöphel to write in his book. Finally, he asked me, "Did the Tibetan government murder Gendün Chöphel?" I replied that they didn't. He said, "Yes, they did. It was clearly mentioned in a book written by a foreign writer." I explained to him, "Lobzang Tenzin-la, you can write in your book that what was written in that particular book was incorrect, and you can explain what is correct. We saw what happened with our own eyes." At the time, I explained to him clearly everything about this, but I am not sure whether or not he wrote it in his book[2].

I was not present at Gendün Chöphel's funeral. Sonam Topgyal came and asked me to make a funeral offering, and I made the offering. Horkhang and most of the aristocrat government officials who were close to Gendün Chöphel made offerings. Sonam Topgyal conducted all the funeral rites. He personally went to deliver the body to the cemetery ground located to the east of Sera. He had brought back with him the skull of Gendün Chöphel. One day, showing the skull to me, he said, "I have kept the skull of my precious teacher. Do you find any special features on it?" "I don't find any special signs on it, but since it is a skull of a lama, you can keep it as the representation of a blessing," I advised.

Sonam Topgyal was born at Rabten Khangsar, which was located near Rampa to the south of Lhasa. He later went to China with Fanjio, in the first group of Tibetans from Lhasa to go to China.

When Gendün Chöphel was alive, many people used to visit him. However, none of us attached any value to his words. Sometimes, he would sing the prayer of Tara and weep at the same time. At other times, he used to tell us incidents that I feel uncomfortable to relate here in front of you, Rinpoche [interviewer Kirti Rinpoche]. He told us stories about his meeting a Japanese girl, a foreign woman, an Indian spy and so forth that made us burst out laughing. For example, he once told us the following incident that happened to him when he was staying in a big hotel in India:

> An Indian man came up to me and looked me up and down from head to foot. I thought he must be a spy, because otherwise he would not look at me in this way. In response, I also looked him up and down. After that, we met several times. *(Alak Jampel: Gendün Chöphel told us in Tibetan; I don't know how he conversed with him in English.)* The man said to me, "Sir, why have you come here?" I replied, "Why have you come here? I have come here to do a work." After that, he followed me wherever I went. One day, when I was walking along in a village, I saw a small teashop with a thatched roof. I stopped there to drink tea. The Indian man also there and said to me, "Have you come here? Where are you going?" I replied, "I am going over there to do a very important thing." Then he said, "What important things do you have to do?" I retorted, "I cannot

tell you everything." After that, I continued my journey and reached a field, with trees and rocks all around. He appeared there again and asked me, "Sir, what are you doing here?" I responded, "I am doing some drawings." "What kinds of drawings are you doing?" he inquired. I said, "I cannot show you everything I have drawn." He again asked, "You have many important things to do, have you?" When I answered, "Who has no work to do?" his face became red. I thought this was not going very well. *(Alak Jampel: Gendün Chöphel used to make fun of others. However, the man was actually planning to kill him.)* I said to him, "You have been following me wherever I go and asking me many questions. What is your purpose?" He answered, "I cannot tell you right now who I am. You are visiting various places, aren't you?" I said, "If you suspect me, come and check me, I shall show you." He looked at my drawings, and said, "I see! These are what you have drawn?" "Yes," I said. He asked, "Oh, I see. Your bag contains these kinds of things? Do you have any other important things in your bag? Can you show them to me?" I said, "I have important things in it, but you can have a look at them." He hesitated and did not touch my bag, but I opened it and insisted that he looked. I showed him everything one by one. I showed him the drawings of an elephant, a monkey and others; he looked at them carefully one by one. Then he put his hand into his pocket and showed me a pistol, and said, "This is the purpose. You can go now." After that, the man never appeared again around that place.

Gendün Chöphel was very clever and always made fun of others, but sometimes he got into trouble because of his suspicious manner. He told me another story:

> One day I went to a big restaurant. An English girl came and said to me, "Welcome. We shall sit together as there are not many people here. You must be tired. I will order tea and cake for you." She went and came back with tea and cakes. We had them together. After a while, she said, "I shall order food for you." I doubted that she was going to deceive me. We did not know each other, so why should she pay for my tea and food when I had enough money? But I said, "Okay." We ate our food together and chatted. Then she said, "Wait a moment here. I have to meet someone. I shall go and come back quickly." I thought, "She wants to leave by tricking me but she did not know how to do it." I said, "Okay." She left, never to return.

He used to tell us such irrelevant stories when he was staying in Garushak building. Many people used to visit him there. He was a learned man and many students would come to him, but he was unable to guide them. In normal practice, a teacher will teach his students one by one as they come. However, Gendün Chöphel seemed to be uninterested in teaching lessons. If one of his students, for example Lobzang Yeshi, came, he would say, "Please come inside and sit for a while, I will teach you in a moment". After a while, when another student came, he would say the same to him. In this way, after a while many students would gather there, but there was no tuition at all; he would just start narrating his own stories.

In India, he wandered about everywhere. On one occasion, he told us the following story:

> One day I went to a brothel in Calcutta. There was a beautiful Japanese girl, whom I liked. I slept with her, and we drank cold drinks and alcohol together. *(Gendün Chöphel did many funny things like this.)* I thought I was having great fun and pleasure. She got up and threw something down on the floor. In fact, she had thrown down the condom with all my semen. I felt disappointed that we had not touched each other in reality.

In general, in terms of nationalistic sentiment, no one was above him. He once told us:

> During the period of the Tibetan Buddhist kings, Tibet had no parallels in the world in terms of military strength and power. This is mentioned even in the histories of foreign countries including Britain. However, such facts are on the verge of disappearing from the country's history. Tibet has a glorious history, which is very valuable, even from the perspective of world history. However, no one is taking care of it. As for other people, they will claim other countries as their own and try to rule them. However, we Tibetans try to exclude everything from us, saying, "This does not belong to us. This is not ours either." So how can our country become powerful? It cannot, can it! Khampa people are called "Khampa rojorwa," (*rojorwa* means embalmer) and they are treated as if they are not Tibetans. Amdo people are called "Amdo beggars" as if Amdo people do not belong among Tibetans. If an Apohor (nomadic Tibetans living in northern Tibet) is seen, he is scorned as "Hor people".

The people of Tsang are called "Tsang-dum-pa", considering them as non-Tibetans. Going further up, there is Lhoka, and its people are nicknamed "Da-kong A-dar" and are excluded. Ultimately, just a small area between Gampa Lamo and Karla is left. Again, within this, the people are differentiated as Khampa traders and so on. So if we consider everything, it gives us the impression that only the Tibetan aristocrats are the real Tibetans. In fact, our people are too eager to exclude others.

In desperate times, we need power. How can we gain power? Just like foreign countries do, we have to bring all our people together. In order to unite our people, we don't have to follow the method used by foreigners. Foreigners use military power to claim other territories as their own. They spend money. We Tibetans do not have to do that. We do not have to send troops. We can just distribute protection cords *(ljags mdud)* or blessing pills from His Holiness the Dalai Lama to our people. These can be sent to Domé through their local rulers. This can be done with Kham also. Everyone will agree to live under the rule of the Tibetan government and no one will raise any objections. Lately, things are not being done correctly. Therefore, when you officials reach higher posts such as senior secretaries, you should remember this. It is very important to have unity among all Tibetans and become one. Just distributing a representation of a blessing from His Holiness can do it. We neither have to spend anything nor do we have to fight a war. It would be good if such things happened in your lifetimes.

Sometimes, when a large group of people including Kungo Lobzang Yeshi and Horkhang's son gathered around him, he would start giving lectures. One day, Horkhang's son said to him in jest, "How about setting up an association called Gendün Chöphel's Association?" He said, "It will be nice. If an association called Amdo Gendün Chöphel's Association is created and everyone is united, it will be very good."

Gendün Chöphel ultimately wished for the unity of all the Tibetan people and for the whole of Tibet to become a single entity. He spoke a lot on such topics. By that time, China had already started proclaiming Tibet as a part of China, and Tibet was on the verge of political turmoil. So, he told us many things that were related to political issues. He once told us:

The Chinese say that religions are a hindrance to politics. Burma sent an invitation to China to send a delegate on the occasion of Burma's Independence Day. A delegate was sent there. On the day of the final ceremony the Chinese delegate was asked to give a speech on how Burma could make progress. He said, "Burma cannot develop because there is not a single Burmese man or woman who has never once taken ordination. People's attachment to religion will hinder the progress of the country. Religion should be sidelined and more effort should be made for the political development of the country. We Chinese have removed the half the monk population of our country—so we were able to defeat Japan." At this, the Burmese got angry and asked him to stop giving the speech and to get down from the stage. It was during the time of the Kuomintang. Nowadays, in the period of Communist China, there is no religion at all. They say that religion will create a hindrance to the governance of the country, and that religion and polity are almost completely antagonistic to each other, like hot and cold. However, the fact is that with the spread of religion, the political state of the country improves instead of declining. There are many instances to prove this.

In Tibet, religion spread during the time of Songtsen Gampo. During his time, the Tibetan empire extended, touching the River Ganga in the south up to Gobi Desert *(bye ma ske ring)* in the north, and this was only because of religion. If there had been no religious influence, Tibet would not have expanded so greatly. Tibetans would not have taken any interest in expanding their empire, apart from fighting wars occasionally with China, with whom she had close relations. In order to spread religion in Tibet, the religious king Songtsen Gampo asked for two images of the Buddha from China and Nepal, and thus he was able to establish a relationship with these two big powers. During the time of the Dharma king Trisong Deutsen, on the advice of the great master Padmasambhava, he sent a large troop of cavalry led by Padmasambhava to invade India. That was also a mission related to religion. This story tells us how the political affairs of a country develop with the spread of religion in the country. It is therefore wrong to say that political status will decline as religion spreads.

He told us that there were different kinds of expansionism. He explained to us:

Tibetan expansion was influenced by religion, because the Tibetan empire grew on religious grounds. The expansion of Mongolia was "military expansion", because they waged wars and conquered territory as far away as France. The British expansion was "expansion caused by famine". In Britain, when the agricultural products of one year were collected and distributed among the people, they could last for only six months, and for the remaining six months, they had to obtain food from outside. Therefore, they first made hammers and sold them as they had an abundance of iron in their country. They exchanged hammers for gold with other countries. When they became familiar with a particular country, they invaded it. They started conquering other countries in order to ameliorate the famine in their own country. Tibet expanded due to religion. To take another example, Christianity is the most widely spread religion in the world. Most of the Christian countries are powerful.

Then he also told us about communism and non-communism. Many say that Gendün Chöphel was a supporter of communism, but that is not true, because he used to speak against it. He said:

[Karl] Marx, the founder of Marxism, was not Russian. He never had a full stomach in his lifetime. He was a very unlucky man who always met with failure in his life. He was jealous of rich people; he planned to distribute their wealth among the poor people in order to bring about economic equality. He founded "Marxism". The reason why communism became popular in Russia is that for twelve consecutive years the harvests in Russia were very poor, which caused a shortage of food in the country. While the wealthy people had everything, the majority of the people faced great hardship. The poor people initially survived by begging food from the rich. The beggars gradually grew in number and strength, and started robbing the rich, resulting in intense and violent clashes between the rich and the poor. Russia was ripped apart by internal strife. The world adopted the wrong policy at that time. Had the USA, Britain and others helped Russia with food and economic aid, the country would not have become communist. At that time, the USA and Britain sneered at them and did nothing to help them. So Russia finally adopted communism and later posed a threat to the world. The USSR became one nation with 32 federal states. When all these states combined and became the communist USSR, it began to pose a grave danger to the world.

So, from his words, it seems that he was not in favour of communism. He told me several times about his arrest by the Tibetan government. He said:

> I met a Chinese man in Calcutta, who asked me to make maps of Assam and Nepal. I did not know whether it would be a good or a bad thing, but I made a map, similar to a military map, which was detailed and easy to read. It contained the names of various places, bridges, villages, police stations mentioning the exact number of policemen in each of the police stations, etc. The British seized the map and they nearly arrested me. Finally, they issued a notice to me demanding that I leave India. After I left India for Tibet, the British government of India sent a letter to the Tibetan government stating that a communist had left for Tibet. Everyone trusted their statement and considered me a communist. I was therefore arrested and imprisoned. The British did this to take revenge on me. The main person behind my arrest was Kashöpa, though there were others also. Later when I was freed from prison, Kashöpa invited me to his house for a meal and made me sit on a high seat. At that time, instead of thanking him, I said to him, "You arrested me. Today you are doing something nice to me. In fact, you were responsible for my imprisonment."

Gendün Chöphel was imprisoned at Zhöl prison. Since he found it difficult to pass the time in prison, he took to drinking to while away the time. He used to drink *chang* (Tibetan brew) as well as alcohol. This was the main thing that ruined his life. Later he told me, "Because I was friendly with the prison guard, he would bring me whatever I asked for. My habit of drinking began at that time."

The British seized his manuscripts on the history of Liyul (Khotan) and sent them to the Tibetan government. Not understanding the texts, the Tibetan government gave them to the prison guard so that he could ask Gendün Chöphel to explain their meaning. After his release, he told me, "I told the prison guard that they (the manuscripts) were of no use to him, but that I would explain them. I explained the meaning (of the texts) to him and he in turn would have told the government officials." Later a text called *An Ornament to Nagarjuna's Intent (klu sgrub dgongs rgyan)* was published. It was reportedly composed by Gendün Chöphel and the contents were against the view of the Geluk

School. As a result some Gelukpa lamas said that he was non-Buddhist. The work was authored by Gendün Chöphel and was published by Dawa Zangpo, with ink and papers provided by Düjom Rinpoche. I doubt that all the views expressed in this book were those of Gendün Chöphel, because he was not the type of person who stubbornly clings to one particular view and refutes others. I can swear that he was not this type of person. I can assure you that not all the views expressed in the book were those of Gendün Chöphel.

Dawa Zangpo was from Nyarong and lived at the Barkor in Lhasa. He used to visit Gendün Chöphel to learn poetry. He was was dull, not intelligent. He studied poetry for only about fifteen days in my presence. He might have also studied with him during my absence. He could not have become expert in poetry and others after studying for only one year, as did Longdöl Lama Rinpoche *(klong brdol bla ma rin po che)*. Though he said he completed the book, we should not believe him blindly. One day when some Geluk lamas whom I knew and I were at my friend's house, they spoke out against the book, saying that it had brought a lot of harm to them. I said, "You must not believe in Dawa Zangpo. The *An Ornament to Nagarjuna's Intent* was based on *Prajnamula (Fundamental Treatise on the Middle Way called Prajna)*". You can ask him how many parts it has and the contents of the each section and their meanings. I am sure he will not be able to explain it; he will make a fool of himself. If you don't believe me, ask him tonight. Tell me tomorrow whether what I have said now is true or not." That night they went to Dawa Zangpo. The next day when we met, I asked them if Dawa had explained it well. They had nothing to tell me except for some funny things that happened that night. Gendün Chöphel made some mistakes in this regard, but it is not that he was not a learned scholar.

Kungo Ngawang Dhondup[3] studied poetry with Gendün Chöphel. When Kungo Ngawang showed his exercises to him, he was not able to make notes on it as his hands were shaking. When we were at the monastery, both the teacher and students had to hold their texts in front of them when the teacher was explaining the text. On the other hand, when Gendün Chöphel was teaching, he never read the text, and only Kungo Ngawang would read the text. If he had to consult a text, he would open a thick Sanskrit book. He had such a high level of knowledge of Sanskrit. He would read only Indian texts for reference, not Tibetan texts. We saw him doing that.

His Tibetan handwriting was so peculiar that it was difficult to differentiate from his English handwriting. [The Kashag] might have given his manuscripts and notes to Kashöpa's son to examine them. When they read his English notes, they understood nothing. They could understand a little from his Tibetan documents. So, they concluded, saying "Gendün Chöphel is patriotic; he has composed a history of Tibet. He is good, not bad." The truth about him ultimately came to light that time.

Gendün Chöphel knew mainly three languages: Tibetan, English and Hindi. Once during our conversation, he said:

> There are some people in Sikkim and other places who boast of knowing eleven different languages. However, in practical terms none of these langauges can serve his purposes—it is just for the sake of claiming to know these languages. If you want to study languages, you should learn these three main languages: the first one is your own language, then English and then any other language. If you learn these three languages, you can put them to practical use. You should learn and become proficient in them before you reach the age of forty. In addition to these three languages, you can learn any other language to a workable level. If you learn a fourth language, for say ten years, you will find no time to use it. So these three languages are the most important.

I would like to clarify one thing here. There is a dictionary that was said to be compiled by Horkhang Geshe Chödrak. In the author's note, it says, "Geshe Chödrak, who was born in Mongolia and has spent his whole life in the land of Tibet, composed the dictionary." Actually the dictionary was compiled by Gendün Chöphel. Horkhang Geshe was popular in those days. He was from Outer Mongolia. He did not have faith in Buddhism and believed in the communist ideology. He once took a revolver from his pouch and said, "Many speak about the protector "Three Jewels". For me this is my real protector. If I keep this in my pouch and go anywhere—mountains, narrow roads, rivers—this will definitely save me." His nick- name was Geshe Jedrakpa *(bye brgag pa)* "non-Buddhist Geshe," and he was also called Horkhang Geshe Chödrak as he served as tutor to Horkhang's son. Later when he sat for his Geshe's examination, he was sarcastically called "The holder of the first division from the bottom." On the day of the debate exam, he invited Horkhang's son as a guest, and told other geshes not to put difficult questions to him, as his patron would witness the exam. However, the other geshes deliberately asked him tough questions. We can see that he was a real self-promoter. I saw him visit Gendün Chöphel often carrying a fountain pen. Gendün Chöphel might have asked him to complete his dictionary. Once I saw Gendün Chöphel giving him instructions regarding the page format of the dictionary. Finally, Geshe Chödrak printed and published the book, which made people believe that he was the author. It can be proved that the dictionary was not his work.

Gendün Chöphel had composed a poem which he used to sing in the same manner he did with the prayer of goddess Tara, in front of his students. The song was:

> *skyid la sdug pa'i 'jig rten mi yul 'dir//*
> *shi yang phyi mig blta ba'i re ba yis//*
> ...
>
> (In this world exists both happiness and sorrow,
> I wish to look back at it even after my death;
> ...)

He had composed antoehr verse which he called "Lament":

> *gzhon dus dga' ba'i chung ma ngas ma blangs//*
> *rgas dus dgos pa'i nor rdzas ngas ma bsags//*
> *sprang po'i mi tshe lcags smyug lhan cig tu//*
> *rdzogs pa 'dis ni bdag gi snang ba skyo//*
> (I did not keep a beloved wife in my youth;
> I did not amass wealth that I need in old age;
> I feel sorrow as this impoverished man
> Is dying, holding a fountain pen in his hand!)

Horkhang Geshe has written that he composed the above verses. If he were to be believed, his poems were used by Gendün Chöphel. However, Gendün Chöphel was not such a desperate man. This is one reason.

Here is another story to prove what I am saying. In 1959 when I arrived in Kalimpong after Tibet had lost its independence, I took up a teaching job. I met Tharchin Babu, and when I asked him about the dictionary, he told me that Gendün Chöphel had taken away his manuscript and never returned it to him. When I asked how they had started the dictionary, he explained, "First we two talked about compiling a Tibetan dictionary and we decided to jointly compile one. We agreed to collect words beginning from the first Tibetan letter "ka". I collected words starting from "ka." Gendün Chöphel also collected some words in the same way. We compared all the lists of words and combined all of them; it became a clear draft. We felt very happy and agreed to continue our work. Then Gendün Chöphel said to me, "You can continue your work and I will also continue with my work. I shall take this manuscript for editing and then return it to you." He took the manuscript to Tibet; my manuscript disappeared in that way."

This is a very clear proof that the dictionary was Gendün Chöphel's work. Nowadays, although he is the real author of the work, the credit is given to someone else.

Gendün Chöphel might have shared with others his views expressed in his *An Ornament to Nagarjuna's Intent*, but he would never say anything that would cause controversy among the different Buddhist schools of Tibet. I have not seen his work *Shakuntala (bya len ma'i rtog brjod)*, but he used to tell us briefly about its contents. For example, he explained to us how a grazing wild animal would act when it was startled by a sudden sound, and how the grass in its mouth would fall out and so on. But, we did not take much interest in it. He told me that an Indian man named Rahul was his friend. I did not ask him how they became friends.

He did not like English people. He said, "The British are the roosters of the world. They make the first call. Even in the political sphere, they are the first to make a prophecy. They interfere in the political affairs of other countries and make decisions."

He had a wife whose name was Yako Lenpar *(g.yag mgo lan par)*. In Lhasa, the name Lenpar referred to prostitutes, because Waku Lenpar and Phorok Lanpar, for examples, were both prostitutes. She had nothing of her own; she was cared for and supported by Gendün Chöphel. With a square face and protruding cheeks, she looked like an *apohor* (dirty and unkempt)[4]. She was from Chamdo.

Gendün Chöphel received money as offerings from his students. He used the money to buy rations. He received monthly allowance from the government in the form of grain and money, but since he got them only at specified times, he was always facing financial problems. His wife possibly did not give him enough liquor. One day when I went to see him at his house, he was overjoyed to see me and said, "Oh, very good, Alak has come." Yako Lenpar said, "Alak has come at the right time; we should decide today." They had quarreled and fought. He said, "She beat me. You see these bruises and wounds. Now I don't need her at all. Please do something to send her back to where she came from." He insisted I send her off. I said, "Don't act in this way. Quarrels between husband and wife are common." He insisted, "I cannot bear this any longer. Please do something to make her go. Please try to arrange the expenses for her to travel from Lhasa to Chamdo." However, I alone was not able to solve the problem, so I went to his students and told them the whole story. They suggested that it would be best to send her away. We made a plan about how to send her. The next day, he and his wife came to me, and said, "Please don't get angry. Yesterday I requested that you send her away. But now, please don't send her away." When Gendün Chöphel died, she was at his house.

I think he was called Alak Dhitsa when he was Labrang Tashikhyil Monastery. If we trace his Nyingma lineage, his father was perhaps of the lineage of a Nyingma lama. Gendün Chöphel first joined Labrang Tashikhyil, and then moved to Drepung Gomang Monastery. He was in the lower class. In the upper class were about 15 Mongolian monks, such as Gen Ngawang Nyima *(rgan nga dbang nyi ma)*, Lekden *(legs ldan)* and Zhiwa Lha *(zhi ba lha)*, who were considered bright students.

The monastery used to hold a debate among the classes in every fourth month each year. The upper and the lower classes had to be questioner or defender in the debate on a rotational basis. One time it was upper class' turn to defend and the lower class to put questions. Gendün Chöphel was in the lower class. Even though we defenders jointly argued him with reapid answers, and even pushing him outside, holding firm with whatever points we put forward, he would defeat us through his simple but sharp and intelligent questions. Even when he was acting as defender, he would give us simple but intelligent answers that would put us in a difficult position. He became popular at Gomang College because of his excellent debating skills. During debate sessions, all the geshes of the monastery, even if they were at the Upper and Lower Tantric Colleges, had to come. The debates were held in the middle of the courtyard and all the learned masters of the Gomang College would sit in the courtyard in a circle. The debate would decide whether one was an expert or not, and Gendün Chöphel made his name at that time.

In the field of drawing and painting too, Gendün Chöphel was superb. In India, once when an Indian spy followed him, he was actually making drawings. He often visited Sonam Topgyal, son of Rabten Khangsar. Sonam Topgyal had a two-storied house. On the wall of the first floor, Gendün Chöphel had drawn a painting of a man riding on a horse. The painting had been made in such a way that the picture looked as if it was protruding from the wall. Gendün Chöphel had an art student called Amdo Jampa. As far as I know, Amdo Jampa was probably at that time a servant of His Holiness the Dalai Lama at Norbulingka. Sonam Topgyal also could draw and paint a little.

My first acquaintance with Gendün Chöphel took place in 1948. His house was very poor—there were only three cushions and a simple kitchen. [His wife] Yako Lenpar's bed and things were kept in the kitchen. The house was very spacious; one side was all covered with windows. On the wall above his bed, he had hung a large scroll painting of Green Tara. The deity looked similar to Palden Lhamo deity—it had three eyes and was seated on a lotus and a moon. I offered him a large red blanket and after that he would always wrap himself in it without wearing anything underneath. In the morning he would not wash his face and offer *yon-chab* (water offering) to the images. He was a real yogi. He would just get up and wear the blanket. His head and hands would shake. Without drinking liquor, he would not be able to speak even a word. He would be stuck with just saying "Ah... ah..." After drinking a glass of liquor, he would sit leaning against the wall and remain motionless for a few minutes. Then he would start talking as if he had woken up from a sleep. When his students came, he would not teach them one by one as they came, but would keep them waiting, until many students had gathered there. Then he would start talking about dirty things and his house would be filled with noise and laughter. Students used to offer him drinks. When he was drunk, he could speak in full flow and looked like a normal person, but when he was not drunk he would look as if he had no sense. I never saw him recite any prayers, but I don't know if he did so in our absence. Sometimes, whether he was unhappy or contemplating on goddess Tara, he would sing the Tara prayer in a braying voice.

According to Geshe Sherab Gyatso, Gendün Chöphel was his student, but the latter never told me about this. The two might have become close to each other during debate sessions at their monastery. The debate session was mandatory for all the classes and Geshe Sherab also had to attend it. They most probably got acquainted with each other during debate sessions, although Gendün Chöphel never told me he was a student of Geshe Sherab.

In earlier times, Tibetan military terminology and drill commands used to be in the Chinese language. Later, the Tibetan army adopted the British military terminology. After that, the Tibetan government decided to convert the Tibetan army's drill commands, which were in English, into Tibetan, saying that it was not good to use them in a foreign language. The government assigned the task of translating them into Tibetan to Kashöpa's son and appointed Gendün Chöphel as his assistant. There were drill commands such as "sna ba rnams ral gri 'pyhar" meaning "Officers, raise your sword". Gendün Chöphel said, "I made a little mistake by not including some Amdo and Khampa dialects in them. The Amdo dialect, in particular, is graceful. The drill commands should be graceful and difficult to understand. It would have been good if we had added a few from our Amdo dialect. "Ha ra song", for example, commands everyone to "go straight" and "tshu ra shog" commands everyone to "come straight". The command "dzog go bsgreng" means "ready to fire", and at this command the soldiers should put their fingers in the trigger guards and be ready to shoot. I made a mistake by not inserting some Khampa and Amdo terms into the Tibetan drill commands. The Tibetan command "rgyab sgyur", which means "about turn", sounds very melancholic in tone."

I did not know if he really meant it, as he said this half in jest. The main credit for translating the British military terminology was given to Kashöpa's son, though the job was actually done by Gendün Chöphel.

One day Gendün Chöphel said to us:

> If we compare the Buddhist King Songtsen Gampo and his minister Thönmi Sambhota, the former's achievements were confined to his lifetime only, but Thönmi's achievements have spread far and wide and are still relevant in the world. Because of the Tibetan scripts invented by him, Buddhism has managed to exist intact in Tibet, from Ladakh in the west to the Domé in the east, as well as in Mongolia. Because of the Tibetan scripts, the Tibetan people have been able to live together and have been able to preserve our national identity. If we do not preserve our grammar, many harmful elements will creep into our language and damage our culture. For examples, some pronounce *hrom* for *khrom*, *bag* for *drag*, *be* for *bre*, *re-ko re-ko* for *re-do re-do*, *yin go* for *yin-no* and so on. If experts do not take care of these things, the phonetic system of our ancient language will be lost and it will become difficult for us to understand the Tibetan religious texts. The scriptures will become mere heaps of papers. Our government must support the experts. Without government support, the mere writings of a few experts cannot prove effective. As happened earlier during the time of King Tri Relpachen, the government should standardize, establish and proclaim a uniform language. If this is done, it will benefit the longevity of the teachings of the Buddha and the preservation of the identity of the Tibetan people.

NOTES

1. When the PLA started invading Tibet from eastern borders, many Tibetans from Kham and Amdo fled to central Tibet, where they formed groups in south Tibet and tried to encounter the Chinese.
2. *"mdo smad kyi mkhas pa dge 'dun chos 'phel,"* in *rgyun mkho'i chos srid shes bya gnas bsdus*", Varanasi, legs bshad gter mdzod khang, pp.173-187.
3. Kungo Narkyi Ngawang Dhondup served briefly in the traditional Tibetan government before 1959 and served in the Tibetan exile government since 1960 in various capacities.
4. Apohor people *(a po hor)* are the nomadic people of northern Tibet. They are reputed to be good at making deceitful pretense. The name Apohor is offensive to other Tibetans.

A Short True Account of Gendün Chöphel

*Thönzur Lobzang Tenzin**

Gendün Chöphel once told me that he went to see the temples of Urshang Do Pema Tashi Gephel Tsuglakhang *('ur shang rdo dpe med bkra shis dge 'phel)* (built during the reign of King Tri Ralpachen) and Karchung Dorji Ying at Rama Gang *(dkar chung rdo rje dbyings)* (built during the reign of Mutik Tsenpo) in order to collect information for his book *White Annals*, which he started to compose after he had arrived back to Lhasa from India. He said to me, "The pillars of Urshang do not have any inscriptions. The inscriptions on the pillars of Dorji Ying Temple have not been damaged." Later, shödrung official Chabtsom Chemi Gyalpo *(chab tshom 'chi med rgyal po)* told me that when Gendün Chöphel went to Shigatsé to do research, he helped him with searching for materials. He said that he found a sack of old documents including one titled Casket of Chong gemstone *(nor bu mchong gi sgrom bu)* in the house of Chuwar Pel, who was said to have served as a secretary in Tsangpa King's government, and that he gave the documents to Gendün Chöphel.

After his release from prison, around 1950, under the instruction of the Tibetan government, Gendün Chöphel and Kashöpa's son

---

* Hailing from a family of Thonzur (thon zur) clan, which got its name from being a branch of the Thönmi Sambhota's lineage, Thönzur Lobzang Tenzin started his career as civil servant at young age. He studied poetry, grammar and other traditional Tibetan subjects under Gendün Chöphel. Since 1959 he spent many years in Chinese prison. Later after his release from the prison, he went to China and worked in the field Tibetan culture. He was among the earliest newcomers from Tibet to arrive in India and served in the Library of Tibetan Works & Archives in Dharamsala and in the Private Office of His Holiness the Dalai Lama.

Dhondup jointly translated the British military terminology and drill commands of the Tibetan army into Tibetan.

In 1949, the Regent Taktra sent his secretary Lobsang Yeshi to call Gendün Chöphel to his monastery, where Gendün Chöphel stayed for about a month, translating the daily radio news in English into Tibetan for the Regent.

In 1951, when the Chinese had already arrived in Lhasa, and when he was staying in Kashöpa's house, one day he said to me, "We Amdo people are brave and determined. If only we had had guns and other weapons earlier, we would have fought the Chinese, and they could not have entered Tibet so easily."

He had a statue of the Buddha which was approximately five to six fingers *(sor)* in height. It was brown and dressed in yellow brocade robes. He had tied brownish eyeglasses to the statue with thread and kept it on his altar. He told me that that statue had been given to him by his father as a symbol of family faith and that the glasses had been given to him by his mother.

One day when I went to his house, he had lit a large butter lamp on the altar. I said, "Why have you made a butter lamp offering today?" He replied, "I have a black pet cat that I brought from my prison. It has not been seen for two days. I fear that someone has killed it for its skin. Today I have offered a butter lamp for its death ceremony." A few days later when I went to his house, he said to me with joy, "Luckily, my cat has not been killed; I have found it." He appeared very happy that day.

After that, the government asked him to complete his unfinished work on Tibetan history *White Annals* and gave him grains and money as his salary. He was allotted a set of three rooms on the upper floor of the Garushak in the building of the Agriculture Department of the Tibetan government. One day when I met him at his new residence, he said to me, "The day before yesterday a beggar came to my door to beg food. I gave him the pouch of barley flour *(tsampa)* together with a spoon. When Tsering Youdön (his wife who lived in Lhasa until 1980) came home, she scolded me saying, "It was all right to give him the *tsampa*, but why did you give him also the pouch and the spoon? Now how are we going to prepare *pak (spags)* ?"

Afterwards, Gendün Chöphel fell ill because of a developing abscess in his stomach. I went to see him and found that his condition was serious. I advised him to take medicine properly and to take care with everything. In a melancholic mood he remarked:

> One who should not have been born was born. Now, one who should not die is about to die!

Bibliography

❖

1. Rakra Tethong, *dge dun chos 'phel gyi lo rgyus*, (Dharamsala: Library of Tibetan Works & Archives, 1980), p3.
2. Dobi Sherab Gyatso, *rdo sbis dge bshes shes rab rgya mtshos mdzad pa'i gsung rtsom*, (Qinghai Ethnic Publishing House, 1983), vol.12.
3. Samdong Rinpoche, *Byams brtse*, (Varanasi, 1999), Vol 2, p.192
4. Hortsang Jigmé, *Drang bden gyis bslus pa 'i slong mo pa*. Youtse Publications, 1998, p.204
5. Samdhong Rinpoche, *Byams brtse pod phreng*. Varanasi: Central Institute of Higher Tibetan Studies, 1999, p.145
7. Horkhang Sonam Pelbar, "mkhas mchog dge 'dun chos 'phel gyi rtogs pa brjo pa 'i snang ba" in *Bod ljongs zhib 'jug*, (Sichuan Xinhua Publication, 1993), Vol. 2, p.4.
8. Ibid. p.4
9. Dorje Gyal, *dge 'dun chos 'phel*, (Kansu Ethnic Publishing House, 1997), p.13
10. Ibid. p.20
11. "dge 'dun chos 'phel gyi gsung rtsom" *Gangs can rigs mdzod*, (TAR People's Publishing House, 1990), Vol.1, pp. 6, 4 and 36
12. Ibid. p.40
13. See footnote No. 9. p.52
14. Ibid. p.61
15. Ibid. p.102

16. Dorje Gyal, *dge 'dun chos 'phel*, (Kansu Ethnic Publishing House, 1997) and mkhas dbang dge 'dun chos 'phel gyis gsar rnyed gsung rtsom, (Zhangkang Ling Publications, 2002).
17. Shora Tenpa Dargye, *mkhas dbang dge 'dun chos 'phel mchog gi mdzad rjes rags bsdus*, Norbulingka Institute of Tibetan Studies, 2002, p.2
18. Rika Lobsang Tenzin, *rgyun mkho'i chos srid shes bya gnad bsdus*, (Varanasi, 1972), p.173.

Reference Materials Relating to the Life and Works of Gendün Chöphel

❖

1. Geshe Sherab Gyatso, *Mi 'jigs seng ge'i nga ro: An overview study of Klu sgrub dgongs rgyan*, a compilation of Geshe Sherab Gyatso's Works, vol. 3. mTsho sngon mi rigs dpar skrun khang.
2. Zemé Rinpoche, *Klu sgrub dgongs rgayn gyi dgag lan 'jam dpal dgyes pa'i gtam gyis rgol lan phye mar 'thag pa rag gcod ral gri'i 'phrul 'khorlo*. Delhi, 1972.
3. Geshe Gendün Tenzin of Rebkong, *lTa ba ngan pa'i mun pa sel bar byed pa shes rab nyi ma'i snang ba*, a refutation to Klu sgrub dgongs rgyan, pecha form, woodblock edition.
4. Rika Lobsang Tenzin, *chos srid kyi shes bya gnas bsdus*. Varanasi, 1992.
5. Chukyi Gendün Samten, *rgol ngal wa skyes tshogs rnams skrag par byed pa 'jigs rung stag gi ngar sgra*, Kansu edition.
6. Khyungtrug Lobsang Dhargyal, *Zab mo bdu ma'i bsnyel zin byams brtse 'o ma'i bsang gtor*, Kansu edition
7. Gartse Tenzin, *mTha' bral dbu ma'i don las 'phros pa'i dpyad pa rdo rje'i mtshon cha*, Kansu edition
8. Geshe Tsultrim Gyatso, *Tshad ma'i dka' gnas gsal bar byad pa'i dus kyi me long*, Bejeing.
9. Dorshi Dongdruk Nyemlo, *Log smra'i tshang tshing sreg pa'i lung rigs rdo rje me lce*.
10. Yonten Gyatso, *gDong lan lung rigs thog mda'*, Paris: 1977.

152 *Gendün Chöphel: Portrait of a Great Tibetan Thinker*

11. *A Collected Essays of Tseten Shabdrung.*
12. Rakra Tethong Thupten Choedar,. *dGe 'dun chos 'phel gyi lo rgyus.* Library of Tibetan Works & Archives, 1979 1980.
13. Tseten Shabdrung, *sNyan ngag spyi don*, 1981, Kan su Mi rigs dpe skrun khang.
14. Tseten Shabdrung, *bsTan rtsis kun btus*. mTsho sngon Mi rigs dpe skrun khang, 1982
15. Tashi Dorjee, *The Life of Gendün Chöphel*. In the Ma 'khyog drang thig, 1982, June July issue.
16. *The Collected Works of Geshe Sherab Gyatso.* mTsho sngon Mi rigs dpe skrun khang.1982, vol. 2 and 3,
17. Horkhang Sonam Palbar, "mKhas mchog dge 'dun chos 'phel gyi rtogs pa brjod pa dag pai' snang ba" Bod ljongs zhib 'jug, pp. 3 31
18. Horkhang Sonam Palbar. "mKhas pa'i dbang po dge 'dun chos 'phel rgya gar du byon skabs kyi gnas tshul," sBrang char, 1983.
19. Liu Yui, "Bod rigs lo rgyus mkhas can dge 'dun chos 'phel gyi lo rgyus mdor bsdus," Bod ljongs zhib 'jug, Vol. 4, 1984.
20. *Autobiography of Tseten Shabdrung*, mTsho sngon Mi rigs dpar skrun khang, 1987
21. Genpo Sherab Gyatso. mKhas dbang dge 'dun chos 'phel gyi rnam thar mdor bsdus (forward). *Collected Works of Gendün Chöphel*, 989.
22. Ven. Lobsang Gyatso. dGe chos kyi bod yig dpe bzhi'i 'dod pa la 'gag pa mdzad pa. In the gSum rtags rgyas bshad brda sprod rin chen bang mdzod. Dharamsala: Sherig Parkhang, 1989, p. 16 and onwards..
23. Shawo Tsering. "mKhas dbang dge 'dun chos 'phel gyi snyan rtsom las bsam blo'i rang bzhin skor gleng ba." Bod ljongs zhib 'jug, Vol. 3, p. 67.
24. Ju Kalsang's poems on *Gendün Chöphel, sBrang char*, vol. 3, p. 84.
25. Alak Zhabdrung, Essay on Goelo. *bstan rtsis kun btus* by Tseten zhabdrung. mTsho sngon mi rigs dpe skrun khang, 1990.
26. Shedrub, "Critical Views on the Songtscn Gampo's Death at aged 34." *Krung go'i bod kyi shes rig*, 1990, vol. 4.
27. Gartse Tamdin Gyal's critical views on some of the years mentoned in the *White Annals*. sBrang char, 1990, vol. 2.
28. Sogpo Lobsang Chokdup, *Yig bshad gsar pa'i lam mkhas pa'i 'khrulspong rigs pa rtogs ldan pa qu'i dpyod yul*. Dharamsala: Library of Tibetan Works & Archives.

29. Introduction to Sonam Palbar (author). Works of Gendün Chöphel, Vol. 1. Bod ljongs yig rnying dpe skrun khang, 1990.
30. Dongthog Tenpai Gyaltsen, Preface: A Self Voicing Truth to the 3rd Edition of Literary Works of Gendün Chöphel, 1991.
31. Drongbu Tsering Dorjee, "Introduction to ten Thinkers from the Land of Intelectuals." *Bod ljongs zhib 'jug,* 1991, vol. 4.
32. A Brief Account of Gendün Chöphel. *Bod kyi lo rgyus g.yu yi 'phreng.ba, part 2,* Bod jong yig rnying dpe bskrun khang, 1991
33. Tsojung Rigpai Lodo,. "Critical views on some of the dates and years mentioned in the *White Annals*". Bod ljongs zhib 'jug, 1991, p 41, 3rd series.
34. Ju Kalsang Choephel's poems on Gendün Chöphel published in *sBrang char,* 1991, Vol 3, p. 84.
35. Tsongkha Lhamo Tsering. *bTsan rgol rgyal skyob*. Amye Machen,1992.
36. Shawo Tsering,"mKhas dbang dge 'dun chos 'phel dang khong gi snyan rtsom bshad pa lhag bsam 'o ma'i rdzing bu, in *Bod kyi shes rig dpyad rtsom phyogs bsgrigs,* Krung go'i bod kyi shes rigs dpe skrun khang, 1992, vol 3.
37. Bushi Sampai Dhondup, "dGe 'dun chos 'phel dang bod kyi lo rgyus zhib 'jug skor rags tsam gleng ba." *Krung go'i bod kyi shes rig,* 1995, vol.2, p. 35.
38. Jinpa Dhargyal,"A Short Essay on Gendün Chöphel's Contribution for Domey and Kham," in *Gang ljongs rig gnas,* 1995, vol.1.
39. "A Brief Account of Gendün Chöphel." *Krung go'i bod ljong zhib 'jug,* 1995, vol. 4.
40. Nordang Ugyan. "On Tibetan famous writer Gendün Chöphel." *Bod kyi rtsom rig sgyu rtsal,* 1995.
41. *Biography of Taklha Phuntsok Tashi,* vol. 1. Dharamsala: Library of Tibetan Works & Archives, 1995.
42. Chabpel Tseten Phuntsok, "A Brief Account of Life of Scholar Gendün Chöphel." *Krung go bod ljongs,* 1996, vol. 4.
43. Ngawang Choedrak, "dBu ma klu grub dgongs rgyan dang 'grel ba'i gzhung gi don gnad 'ga' la rags tsam dpyad pa", *Bod ljongs zhib 'jug,* 1997, issue No 3, p. 60.
44. "Shes rab rgan po'i 'bel gtam." *sBrang char,* 1997, issue No 3, p. 112.

45. Yeshi Gyatso's poems on Gendün Chöphel published in *lJon zhon*, 1997, issue No 9, p. 82.
46. Dorje Gyal, *dGe 'dun chos 'phel*. Kansu Mi rigs dpe skrun khang, 1997.
47. Introduction to the "Collected Essays of Gendün Chöphel". *Krung go'i bod kyi shes rig de*, 1998 issue No 3, p.157.
48. Hortsang Jigmey, *Drang bden gyis bslus pa'i slong mo ba*, Youtse ,1998.
49. Sakar Woeser, "dGe chos ka rtsom gyi mchan bu a mchod mgul rgyan." *Nor 'od*, 1999 vol. 1 & 2, p. 20.
50. Prof. Samdong Rinpoche, Introduction to *gTam rgyud gser gyi thang ma'i klad*, 1999.
51. Rakra Tethong Thupten Choedar, *rGyal rabs deb ther dkar po'i kha skong mes blon gong ma'i zhal chems*, Library of Tibetan Works & Archives, 2001.
52. Gedün Lhundup's poems on Gendün Chöphel published in *sBrang char*, 2000 issue 4, p.89.
53. Dungkar Lobsang Thinley, "Gendün Chöphel," in *Dung kar tshigs mdzod*. Krung go Bod rigs pa'i dpe skrun khang, 2002, p. 604.
54. Alak Shabdrung's reply to the *White Annals*' claim that Songtsen Gampo died at Age 34. *Collected Essays of Tseten Zhabdrung*. mTsho sngon Mi rigs dpar skrun khang, p.166.
55. Danma Lobsang Dorjee, *Rigs dang khyab bdag rgya mtsho'i he ru ka: dPal ngur smrig gar rol skyabs gcig pha bong kha pa bde chen snying po dpal bzang po'i rnam par thar ba don ldan tshangs pa'i dbyangs snyan*, Lhasa: woodblook edition.
56. *Bod kyi rigs gnas lo rgyus rgyu cha bdams bsgrigs*, vol. 3.
57. Jigmey Phuntsok Jungney, *Dus rabs nyer gcig pa' gangs can la phul ba'i snying gtam sprin gyi rol ma*. Moser Nyingma Monastery.
58. *Life History of Sampho Tenzin Dhondup*. Dharamsala: Library of Tibetan Works and Archives.
59. *Gangs can mkhas grub rim byon gyi ming mdzod*. Kan su Mi rigs dpe skrun khang.